SPOKANE HOUSE IN THE AUTUMN OF 1839 (Sketched from memory.)

A BRIEF HISTORY

OF

SPRINGVILLE, UTAH,

FROM ITS FIRST SETTLEMENT

SEPTEMBER 18. 1850. TO THE 18th DAY OF SEPTEMBER. 1900

FIFTY YEARS

"Blow ye the Trumpet. Blow. for the Year of Jubilee"

COMPILED AND WRITTEN BY

DON CARLOS JOHNSON

PRINTED BY
WILLIAM F. GIBSON. SPRINGVILLE
SEPTEMBER. 1900

PUBLISHED BY

D. C. JOHNSON & WM. F. GIBSON

SPRINGVILLE, UTAH

INTRODUCTORY

THE writing of the following pages is undertaken partly as a labor of love, and partly to publish some of the more important items of the history of Springville before those who know the facts shall have passed away, and to preserve for the use of the rising generation a narrative of the trials of the fathers and mothers in the early settlement of our city: in subduing the desert, and in conquering the many obstacles encountered in the home-making of fifty years ago. Soon all of the old-timers will have passed over the border into the Land of Shadows. Probably before another decade has passed away none will be with us of "The Old Folks" who experienced the vicissitudes of pioneer life in this valley. Some of those who held the plow to turn the first furrow, and cracked the lash over the backs of the patient oxen, are still with us: also some of the dear mothers who toiled patiently beside the fathers are yet left to tell the story.

It is the Author's desire to make the narrative interesting and impartial. He has consulted the survivors, and from their statements of facts, and some written data from the Journal of Aaron Johnson, this history is compiled. The early records are very incomplete. none having been kept by the "Branch" in regular order until the year 1870. at the time Bishop Bringhurst was appointed. Some minutes of the Teachers' meetings. kept by Joseph D. Reynolds and John M. Clemments. and a record of the Black Hawk War kept by William Bramall. who had charge of the commissary department. have been found valuable in fixing dates. This history is not written to give undue prominence to any person or persons. but to deal justly with all. In such a brief space every particular happening cannot be fully dealt with. but the endeavor shall be to in a general way record the prominent events in the order of their occurrence. giving accuracy as to date. and fidelity as to statement.

There are among all peoples a little band of leading spirits whose memory is especially enshrined in the hearts of their descendants: they who have ushered in some new order of things: perhaps by defying a tyrant's power by force of arms. laying down their lives to maintain a sacred principle and transmit the same to their children as a heritage much to be prized: perhaps by penetrating some hitherto unknown country of desert and wilderness, to open it for settlement and for the establishment of the arts of peace and civilization. Coming nearer to our own time, we delight to honor and give praise to the memory of our own pioneers—the first settlers of Springville. They were pioneers in very deed, in many states and territories. Many of them penetrated the undeveloped West, and made several homes. All of our pioneers came from the older states, and by successive stages arrived in the land of Utah to make their future and final earthly homes. The Millers, Crandalls, Birds and Sanfords came from "York State;" the Johnsons and Halls from Connecticut: the Mendenhalls from Delaware and the Deals from North Carolina. They all passed through the different phases of the Mormon church: in its meanderings from Kirtland, Ohio, Far West, Missouri, and Nauvoo, Illinois. They made settlements at various places in Iowa during the time between 1846 and 1850. In the latter year they crossed the Plains to Utah, where they found a resting place, and where now their numerous descendants mostly dwell.

As for the pioneers, their days are numbered, their life's work is done, and that it has been well done none will care to dispute. The rude forces of Nature were made subservient to their will, and to minister to our comfort and pleasure. The wild Indian who once owned these fair acres and who roamed at pleasure, hunting and fishing, upon the grassy expanses and beside the streams and lake in our beautiful valley, stands now a melancholy specter up on the horizon, as he is about to disappear forever from the haunts of men. But few of the Red-men remain to tell of the rude race that has been supplanted by the restless and progressive Pale-face. The conquest was inevitable. The two races could not live in the same valley, and as Fate has ordained, the weak gave way to the strong. It has been so from the morning of time. The room of the inferior races has been more desirable than their company, and acting upon this theory the superior races have, with almost ruthless hand, swept everything undesirable to themselves, or that retarded their progress, to the wall.

Not only have the vile reptiles and every noxious thing that creeps and crawls been mostly destroyed, but the beautiful denizens of the forest and plain have been removed to give place to the cattle and other domestic creatures of the civilized home. The canyon torrents which dashed and foamed down between the towering hills, stealing through sun and shade across the beautiful valley, where now our city stands, were turned aside upon the thirsty soil and thus the earth has been made to yield all the fruit and flowers, and foods of man in endless variety and great abundance, or turned upon the mill wheel, made to furnish power for the factories, light our homes and perform many of the labors of men.

Springville lies in the midst of Utah Valley, at the foot of the majestic Wasatch range. Her surroundings are indeed beautiful. Look in whatever direction you will, a landscape meets the eye, to thrill the heart of poet or artist: the surrounding heights with grand variety of peak. pass and summit: the deep, cool canyons from which flow the streams of sparkling water; fields and orchards freighted with their products of fruit. flower and grain: and the beautiful lake. nestling at the foot of the western hills, whose peaks are mirrored in its cool depths. make a picture worthy of the master's brush or pen. What must have been the feelings of the pioneers, when they drove their jaded. faithful teams upon the site of this lovely piece of land fifty years ago. and commenced the city in which we now dwell?

Without further preliminary the Springville pioneers will now be introduced to the reader, and their toils narrated in "making glad the waste places. and the desert to blossom as the rose."

A BRIEF HISTORY

OF

SPRINGVILLE, UTAH,

FROM ITS FIRST SETTLEMENT

SEPTEMBER 18. 1850. TO THE 18TH DAY OF SEPTEMBER. 1900.

CHAPTER I.

AN occasional white man had seen the beautiful Utah valley prior to the permanent settling of the homeseeker. Kit Carson. with John C. Freemont. the "American Pathfinder." had passed through this State and valley in the '30's. and an account of their journey and findings was published in the East. In these observations Provo river was noted: the Great Salt Lake was partly located and surveyed. and the adventurous party sailed upon the waters of Utah lake.

"Old Bridger." a white trapper. with some daring and adventurous spirits. had hunted the wild animals and trapped the beaver and otter upon the streams and along the sedgy borders of the lake. Barney Ward. an old trapper and Indian fighter. had been in this valley for some years prior to the advent of the Utah pioneers. and was here at the time of their arrival. Wm. Wordsworth. one of the pioneers and for many years a resident of this city. came to the Utah valley in the autumn of 1847 and made some observations along the lake border in the northern extremity of the valley: he followed Hobble creek. nearly to the mouth of the canyon. and found the creek bed dry nearly the entire distance. Parley P. Pratt with a party. among whom was George B. Matson. passed through here enroute south on an exploring expedition in 1848.

Coming to our own citizens. Oliver B. Huntington came to this locality with Barney Ward upon a trading expedition in February. 1849. Being young. ardent and filled with the spirit of adventure. he was easily persuaded by the old trapper that there was money in it. and he concluded to do some trading with the natives for peltries. Accordingly several pack animals were loaded with such gew-gaws as would delight the dusky denizens of the valley: notably red flannel. gaudy bandannas. paints. brass rings. powder and shot. beads. etc.—and started for the valley of the Utah lake. At this time the snow lay a foot deep all over the Utah valley. The dry bunch grass protruded from the white crust six inches in many places and afforded excellent feed for their horses. The adventurers only went as far as the Spanish Fork river, where a camp was made for a few days and some thrifty exchange was had with the natives for beaver, otter and deer skins.

At this camp Stick-in-the-Head and Little Chief were encountered. The former was so named because of the mode in which he arranged his hair. His long, luxuriant locks were done up in a bob upon the back part of his crown, and held in place by a grease-wood stick which served the same purpose as the ladies' hairpin of the present day. This bob was a mark of distinction, and served as well for a protection from the stroke of a war-club in the hands of an enemy.

The trading party, returned at the end of the week, and made their camp about the center of Fourth street, near the site of the present residence of William Giles. The horses were hobbled and turned out to feed upon the ripened grasses that grew abundantly in that locality. In the morning the bell-horse had become unhobbled and led the band astray out across the valley toward the mouth of Maple canyon. Mr. Huntington easily followed the trail out through the cedars which grew on what is now known as Mapleton Bench, and soon returned to camp with the runaways. From this incident of the "hobbles" Hobble creek was named, and that name was borne by the settlement for many years.

While on this expedition the traders encountered, in the clay beds between Spanish Fork and Hobble creek, a wick-i-up containing an Indian family, and with it an Indian girl tattooed on the forehead with some savage device. There was also tethered near a beautiful "pinto" pony. Mr. Huntington wanted to trade for the dusky maiden and the pinto, for the purpose of taking them to his native State of New York and selling them to Barnum's circus as curios, and thereby make a stake.

The owner, however, wanted more than he could afford to pay, and the trade was not consummated. Mr. Huntington came in an early day to live at Springville, was one of the early schoolmasters, and has been all these years a toiler for the advancement of our city. It may here be chronicled that he taught the first school in a house with books at Salt Lake City in the winter of 1847-8. A lady had taught, the previous autumn, a sort of kindergarten for the little ones, in a tent and without books.

We now come to the real locator of Springville as a town-site— William Miller. He came to Salt Lake City in September, 1848, and built a home with the intention of remaining there. In February, 1849, news came that the Utes had attacked the fort on the Provo river, and that it was in a state of siege. A force of 200 volunteers was hastily organized and equipped, and marched to the scene of hostilities where they relieved the beleagured fort. Mr. Miller held an official position in that battalion of cavalry. James Mendenhall was also one of those volunteers, and he in connection with Mr. Miller took a trip down through the valley as far as Payson then called Peteetneet, but found no place that delighted them as did the site on Hobble creek. Here they resolved to come with their friends and make a settlement. After returning to Salt Lake City, Mr. Miller communicated his desire to Brigham Young, the spiritual leader of the people, who readily agreed to the scheme. It was then arranged that as soon as Aaron Johnson and his company came to Utah they would be assigned to Hobble creek to make a permanent settlement. In the summer of 1850, while Johnson' company was on the Plains, Mr. Miller brought his wife, Phœbe, down to inspect the proposed home-site. They came, they saw, and were conquered.

Never had their eyes beheld a more

BISHOP AARON JOHNSON.

eligible site on which to make a home. The season was early June, and the scorching rays of the sun had not yet parched the landscape: acres of waving grass, studded with bright colored flowers, beautified the broad expanse from the lake to the snow line on the mountains, and loaded the pure air with their fragrance and bloom.

The rest of the season was spent in preparing for the removal to this locality when their friends should arrive in the Valleys. When Aaron Johnson came into Salt Lake valley on the 2nd day of September, 1850, with his train of 135 wagons, he was met by Mr. Miller, who informed him that his home was already selected for him and that arrangements had been consummated for them to go to Utah valley and form a settlement. After resting and visiting for a few days Miller and Johnson mounted their horses and rode down to Hobble Creek to satisfy Capt. Johnson that no mistake had been made. They examined the country carefully from the "Point of the

Mountain" to this place, but with no place were they so well satisfied as at Hobble Creek. They, while on this trip, rode around and agreed that the future city should stand almost exactly on what was afterward surveyed as "Plat A, of Springville," and returned to their families. Upon their final report to Governor Young, they were called to go to Hobble Creek and make a settlement, with the understanding that Aaron Johnson was to be the District Judge of Utah County, and William Miller Associate Justice.

Brigham Young went down to the Emigration Square where Johnson's company was corralled, and cut out the first eight wagons of the company of which Johnson was captain, and said they were to go to the selected locality and build a fort, which would be merged into a town as soon as would be practicable.

The eight teams comprised those of Aaron Johnson, Myron N. Crandall, John W. Deal, Amos S. Warren and brothers, and Richard Bird. Mr. Bird went up north of the city into Davis

WILLIAM MILLER.

County to visit his brother, James, and on returning remained at Mill Creek to do a little threshing for a brother and did not join his companions until October 1st.

In consequence of some road making it took the better part of three days to make the trip from Salt Lake City to their destination. At this period the teams were compelled to drive over the mountains at Jordan Narrows, instead of around the point as at present.

WILLIAM SMITH'S HOUSE, ONE OF THE OLD FORT ROW

CHAPTER II.

ON the 18th of September, 1850, Capt. Johnson, with the wagons containing the first families, arrived on the future site of Springville, and encamped on the little bluff at the spot where Cyrus Sanford's house now stands, and corralled their wagons. Their long journey of 1,100 miles was over, they had found rest and a place to expend their future energies. For the last five years they had been in a state of unrest and uncertainty, and now all seemed settled so far as their future wandering was concerned.

The train had "nooned" that day at Bullock's Springs, south of Provo, and about 2 o'clock p. m. drove down across the Big Pasture, crossing Spring creek where it is now spanned by the Rio Grande Western railroad bridge. The leading team was driven by Martin P. Crandall, and all arrived upon the old Fort plat at 3 p. m. The location was one of great natural beauty: one to fill the hearts of the weary pilgrims with

JANE SCOTT JOHNSON

oy and thankfulness. The high mountains surrounding the beautiful valley: he tall grasses bending with billowy racefulness to the movement of the utumnal breezes: the flashing, silvery ake which lay shimmering beneath the urple shadows of the cloud crowned ills and the bluest of blue skies bending over all, making altogether a picture never to be effaced from the memries of the delighted homeseekers. The season was the beautiful and hazy utumn, with its enchanting hues covering hill and dale, mountain peak and alley.

The names of those who came he first day are: Aaron Johnson, his vives Jane Scott and Mary Ann Johnon, and his children, Don C., William .. and Aaron: William Miller and his vives, Phoebe Scott, Marilla Johnson nd Emeline Potter, with his adopted ons, George and Heber Chenaworth: Myron N. Crandall, his wife Tryphena nd children, Julia A., Horace O. and Myron E.: John W. Deal, his wife Eliza nd their children, Mary, Daniel E., ohn W., jr., and Laura: Martin P.,

Nelson D. and Lucien D. Crandall: Charles, Amos S. and Mary Warren, and Wellington Wood, a lad of nine years. Richard Bird's family, which was among the first, consisted of his wife Emeline and his sons, R. Leroy and Martin W. Willis K. Johnson, son of Aaron Johnson, died of cholera while crossing the plains and his wife Laura remained in Salt Lake City in consequence of illness, where Willis K. Johnson was born. They came to Springville about the first week in October.

Here is a fitting place to describe the "outfits" in which our city's pioneers crossed the plains from Missouri to Utah. Captain Johnson had three teams, two yoke of oxen on one wagon in which was carried the heavy freight, consisting of a cook stove, plow, material for a harrow and tools necessary for the making of a new home. Two yoke of cows drew the wagon containing the provisions and

MARY ANN JOHNSON

EMMELINE POTTER MILLER

the cooking utensils for the daily use. These faithful cows not only did service as draft animals but their flow of milk never failed. By putting the milk left over from breakfast and dinner in a churn fixed in the hind end of the wagon, butter was churned by the jolting motion and used to oil the campfire pone at mealtime. The other wagon was drawn by a span of horses called "Black and Bay." This wagon was fitted up with a box made on the plan of the sheep wagon of today and was used as a family gathering place, a kind of parlor on wheels. Tradition has it that Aaron Johnson and his brother Lorenzo invented the wagon box with projections. This wagon was built by Captain Johnson just after crossing the Mississippi river in 1846, without one piece of iron in its construction. Rawhide did service as tires and where bands were necessary the same material served, while for king bolt, linch pin and other bolts, hickory wood was used. This wagon and others similar were driven across the plains of Iowa, and then ironed at Council Bluffs, afterward doing many years of faithful service in the valley. The other families came by means of similar transportation. Some saddles, guns and ammunition had been brought along for hunting and to protect them from the Indians who infested the long immigrant trail and mountain wilds. Beneath the stars, which the weary travelers recognized as the same bright luminaries that had always seemed to keep watch over them from their childhood's home in the far East to their new resting place, they would gather every evening around the chief campfire after the shadows had fallen over the landscape, and offer to the God of their fathers heartfelt thanks for their goodly surroundings and cherished prospects of future peace.

Bright and early on the morning of the 19th the hardy pioneers were up and doing. While the mothers and daughters prepared the first meal of the day, the male portion hung grindstones and sharpened scythes, preparatory to the haymaking from the wild

MARILLA JOHNSON MILLER

grasses which grew luxuriantly in every direction. Axes were prepared and wagons were selected to go into the canyons for logs with which to build a fort to protect themselves, not only from the wintry snows which would soon cover the valley but from the wild natives who then roved unmolested in the land.

The fort was built on the rising ground about where the Third ward schoolhouse now stands, and covered one and one-half acres of land. It was constructed to serve as a fortress as well as a home. There were log or block houses around the area, locked together at the corners, with clay roofs over all, and the windows and doors opening into the courtyard. There were two large gates, one in the east and one in the west side, which were the only means of ingress and egress. These gates were flanked by bastions at the corners, so that an enfilading fire could sweep the walls in every direction. In case of an attack the cattle could be driven into the courtyard for security. The logs for the houses were procured up the creek bottom and at the forks of Hobble

creek canyon, where there grew a beautiful grove of cedars and cottonwoods. The cottonwood entered largely into the construction of the walls of the houses, while the cedar, which grew tall and straight and would "split like an acorn," was used for ridge poles, joists and rafters. S. C. Perry, William Smith and Charles Hulett took the first teams into Hobble creek canyon and brought out loads of logs, one load of which entered into the construction of Mr. Smith's house, which stood in the southeast corner of the fort. These logs grew upon the flat at the Forks, were of balsam, and the same timber that is displayed in the log cabin (see page 4) in this work.

After the work of building the fort and hay gathering was well under way other families came in, and barely taking time to say "howdy," took a hand in building the fort and all joined in, working unselfishly for the common good. Before the storms of winter set in the fort was completed, and the pilgrims were once more in a home which was indeed their castle, that protected them from the blasts of winter and from the forays of the painted warrior.

CHAPTER III.

ΑΝ abundance of wild hay was gathered in; cord upon cord of wood stacked by the cabin doors; and every possible preparation made for spending a comfortable winter in their new home. The women and children had, in the autumn months, gathered the ground cherries which grew in abundance everywhere. Merry companies went to the canyons and gathered bushels of "servis" berries and choke berries, which they dried and stored away for the Christmas holidays.

A berrying excursion under the direction of Aaron Johnson went into the

left hand fork of Hobble creek canyon as far as Berry Port, and camped over night on the bench where the Whiting ranch now is. Ten bushels of the fruit were gathered by the deft fingers of the female members of the party, while the men had some experience with the ugly grizzlys that were feasting on the luscious berries. No bear were bagged however, and the party returned to the fort on the second day, without meeting any of the natives, who still hung around and glanced askance at the white intruder.

Before Christmas the following fami-

MYRON N. CRANDALL.

lies had joined the colonists and were assigned quarters in the fort: Spicer Crandall, Horace Spafford, Peter Boyce, Smith Humphrey, John Roylance, Ira Allen, Simeon Blanchard, Cyrus Wingate, James Mendenhall, Jonathan Ford, William Smith, Stephen Perry, Cyrus Sanford, Jackson Stewart, James Dotson, Charles Hulett, Edward Starr, Sylvester Hulett, Nathan Wixman, Hugh D. Lisonbee, Daniel Wood, Edward Zam and George Burton, two U. S. soldiers who deserted from Fort Laramie, and followed Captain Johnson's company to Salt Lake; also Riley Stewart and Charles Ingalls.

Next to be mentioned is Asael Perry, who was the first president of the branch at Springville, and Aaron Johnson was the first bishop. They received their appointments in the winter of 1850-1 from Brigham Young. William Miller and Myron N. Crandall were Johnson's counsellors. There were also three brothers—John, Alex and William Nichols, who were called the "adobe boys," because they made the first adobes in Springville. These adobes

were very large, being 12x18 and requiring two men to handle them. The "adobe boys" built a two roomed house within the confines of the fort, of those adobes. The rooms were large enough to dance two cotillions in and they were used for all social gatherings until the log school house was completed about the new year, wherein the first school in Springville was taught by Cyrus Sanford; and there some now living began their education, fifty years ago. Some claim that Phœbe Miller, a teacher by profession, taught school the first winter and that Mr. Sanford did not teach until the second winter. The school house was seated with puncheons, hewn from cottonwood trees and had two inch pegs for legs. The tables were made from parts of wagon boxes, held together with the old nails taken from them. Paper and pens were very scarce, quills answering the purpose of pens and the ink was made from dyestuffs which the pioneers had brought from the East. There was a great variety of text books, brought

TRYPHENA CRANDALL.

JOHN W. DEAL

and the sweethearts "tripped the light fantastic toe," to the inspiring strains of music furnished by the village fiddlers, Hugh Lisnbee and one of the Nichols boys.

The first child born in Springville was Franklin A. Crandall, who was born the 21st day of November, 1850. He died on the 22nd day of September, 1883, from injuries received in a railroad accident.

The boys of that winter were Elmer Taylor, Nelson Spafford, Spicer, Martin P., Nelson D., and Lucien D. Crandall, Thomas and William Roylance, Hugh D. Lisonbee, Procter Humphrey and the Nichols brothers.

The girls however were not so plentiful; still many of the wives were gay and young and there was no lack of partners at the cotillion parties during the winter, but by the next many other families joined the settlers bringing their daughters, thus making enough to go around. Thus the winter was spent enjoyably and profitably, while

from the old homes—McGuffy's readers, Old and New Testament, Pilgrim's Progress, Æsop's Fables, The Scottish Chiefs, Doctrine and Covenants, and The Book of Mormon were some of the books used. With these and a judicious use of birch switches, the young idea began to grow in this locality.

It was in the Nichols' building that the first marriages were solemnized. Spicer Crandall was the first to lead a bride, Miss Sophia Kellogg, to the altar. They were married by Aaron Johnson. Elmer Taylor was married next to Miss Wealthy Ann Spafford. Next came Nelson Spafford and Emma Johnson. The last named were married by William Miller. On each occasion an excellent feast was spread and all within the fort partook. The healths of the young couples were pledged in bumpers of rustic beverage, all concluding with a cotillion party, where the beaux

ELIZA DEAL

plans for the future were maturing. Meetings, debates and spelling schools formed, the literary pleasures, and cotillion parties with games appropriate for young and old formed the pastimes—all of which helped to pass the long winter evenings and to fully recruit the jaded travelers for the planting time, now rapidly approaching.

Soon Winter was compelled to relax his frozen grip from the valley before the bland smile of the sun and retreat to his northern home. As soon as dry ground appeared a surveying party under Andrew J. Stewart, set to work to complete the survey of the city and farms, which had been begun the autumn before and was completed for the spring planting. This spring William Miller organized a company of mounted minute men as a protection to the settlers and as an object lesson to the Indians, who were camped at several places in the valley and were looked upon by the pioneers with suspicion.

CHAPTER IV.

 N March 3, 1851, the first court opened at Provo with Aaron Johnson as judge. A grand and petit jury was summoned to indict and try any criminal cases that might come before them. There were in the first jury, Peter Boyce, Orrin Craw and Spicer W. Crandall. The first indictment charged one Henry Myers with stealing three horses from Utah Fort. Before court adjourned the following names were selected to sit as grand jurors for the next term of court—Ira Allen, Smith Humphrey, Myron N. Crandall, Edward Starr, Stephen C. Perry, Richard Bird, James Guyman and William Smith.

The first general election was held on August 4th, 1851, in this precinct, which then embraced all the territory from Provo to Spanish Fork, and from the lake border to the base of the mountains. The election was held in the fort school house. The judges of election were, Asael Perry, Orrin Craw and Peter Boyce. At this election William Miller and Aaron Johnson were elected territorial senators. This Legislature appointed Orrin Craw and Mathew Caldwell justices of the peace and Cyrus Sanford as constable. It will be seen that many of our first settlers were given due prominence as officers of the territory and county.

Seed grain had been procured in Salt Lake valley from the pioneers of 1847-8-9 who had quite a surplus, which they sold at $1.00 per bushel. In the beginning small farms of twenty acres were allotted to each as it was believed at that time that not over one hundred families could be maintained in this vicinity upon twenty acre holdings, in consequence of the scarcity of water.

In the spring 1851 there was but one blacksmith shop in the valley, located in Provo. Our pioneers were compelled to go there for their blacksmithing and as there was considerable repairing to be done the shop had orders a week ahead. One anecdote will suffice to illustrate the importance of the blacksmith at that period: Captain Johnson had found some rifle barrels while crossing the plains; any kind of steel being valuable he had brought them along and concluded to make a set of harrow teeth from them by cutting into proper lengths, inserting a piece of steel in the bore, welding, sharpening and then tempering. Richard Bird, also, had an interest in the harrow, and together they went to Provo to have the work done. They arrived at noon and ascertained that the work could not be done for a week and would cost them $5.00. As the smith was removing his apron to go to dinner, he was asked if the forge and tools could be used in his absence. Upon receiving a reply in the affirmative, coats were laid aside and the amateur smiths prepared to do one of the best hour's work of their lives, with Bird at the bellows and Johnson at the anvil. A half bushel of charcoal was heaped on the fire and a dozen barrels were thrust in. The flames roared and rushed up the chimney, while sparks flew from the heated metal as the sledge and lighter hammer fell with lightning like rapidity and the water in the ladling pool fairly boiled as the hot teeth dropped in quick succession into its depths. Just as the smith returned from his dinner, the job was near completion, only a three teeth remaining in the fire awaiting the finishing touches. They had been just fifty-five minutes and the charge for charcoal and the use of the tools was fifty cents. All our pioneers were frontiersmen and handy at all kinds of labor incident to planting the wilderness. There were blacksmiths, carpenters, masons, farmers and some jacks-of-all-trades, but none were familiar with irrigation, only in a general way, though many useful hints were given by the pioneers of 1847.

To Richard Bird and John W. Deal belong the credit of doing the first plowing, in February 1851, in what is now the big pasture. Early in March every team and plow were at work and the grain was soon planted and also some vegetables. After the crops were planted, the water was turned out on both sides of the creek near where it enters the town on the east. John W. Deal was in charge of the men, twenty-six in number, who made the canal on the south side of the stream. Aaron Johnson "bossed" a like number of men with teams, who turned out the creek at the same place where it now runs from the old channel. Their method of leveling was to look over the ground first, then plow one furrow a short distance, clean it out and turn the water in behind, and so on to the end and then turn the water off and then finish the ditch to its proper dimensions. Nearly all the stream was used that year upon the growing crops. The land was so very dry that the water could be but slowly forced over it. Hobble Creek at that time ran through the present town site, in its narrow channel, with tall cottonwood trees interlacing their branches from either side; still there were indications of high water previously. The first summer by the Fourth of July the creek was nearly dry; a man could have easily jumped from bank to bank.

In June a meeting was called to discuss the advisability of celebrating the Fourth of July. However, it was unanimously agreed to defer the celebration until July 24th, because provisions

MARTIN P. CRANDALL

were scarce and by the twenty-fourth vegetables could be had in abundance. Consequently preparations were made for the proper observance of the day. Some of the young men ascended to the grove south-east of town at what is known as the Big Slide for a liberty pole, which they procured and planted in the center of the fort. A spacious bowery was built under which tables were spread and all was ready for the glorious pioneer day.

The day before the 24th Cyrus Sanford and others were at Provo and saw the old cannon, which the pioneers had brought in 1847 and sent to Provo as a defence against the Indians in 1849. While the Provo boys were boasting about how they were going to awaken their Hobble Creek neighbors the next morning with their big gun, the Springville boys were turning over a scheme in their minds to "swipe" the cannon. In the evening, after reaching home, the matter was discussed and they decided to go back to Provo in the night, capture the gun and bring it to the fort. A half dozen young men, anxious for a lark, gathered at the appointed place and set out. The Provo boys were unsuspecting and the gun was easily taken from its place and carted out of town. The boys had not gone far when they found the gun too heavy and unwieldy and they decided to hide it in a cornfield near by. At daylight the next morning the Hobble Creek boys awakened their Provo neighbors with E. O. Haymond's anvil, which made the echoes ring along the mountain tops for the first time on the 24th of July in this valley.

At 9 a. m. the inhabitants of the fort were out in their holiday attire. Having come so lately from the old states, all had still some article of finery. There were ladies in white and men in black while children mingled in the gay crowd, dressed in their new clothes fashioned from their parents' old ones. After the program all were seated at the tables, which were loaded with the products of farm and garden, with wild game in abundance. The tables were decorated with festoons of wild flowers, the whole making a delightful picture. William Miller acted as master of ceremonies and sat at the head of the long table. There are some still with us who remember how he was attired on that occasion. It is asserted that Peter Boyce and William Miller were the best dressed men on that day. A description of the costume of the master of ceremonies will suffice: His trousers were of white linen, fit for a Broadway swell, vest of white, beautifully figured, and a shirt with an embroidered front. His collar was a light silk stock and his gaiters were of morocco. A swallow tail coat completed his costume—the same one he had worn in "York state" years before to the "quiltings." The afternoon was spent in games and the dance was kept up, with a vim and enjoyment seldom equalled, until a late hour.

The harvest was satisfactory this

RICHARD BIRD

year, everything far exceeded their most sanguine expectations. Aaron Johnson's diary records his raising of 600 bushels of wheat, and oats and barley in proportion. Melons and squashes literally covered the ground. The grain was threshed upon the primitive threshing floor, the same kind used by Gideon of ancient fame, and winnowed by the wind. This threshing floor was simply a circular section of ground, leveled and packed hard. In the center was a post with a swivel to which a chain was attached to keep the oxen in place, while they trod out the grain. A load of sheaves was placed around the post, the two yoke of cattle were attached to the center post and driven around in a circle until the grain was shelled. Then the straw was raked off, the chaff and wheat piled aside, until a wind blew strong enough to winnow the grain. Some threshed on wagon covers, using the flail, but all cleaning was done with the aid of the winds.

That autumn consternation seized the more timid ones of the colonists, when, one day two hundred Indian warriors dashed up, gaudy with paint and flying feathers, and camped about one-fourth of a mile west of the fort. They were under the immediate command of Walker, the war chief of the Ute nation. Ammon, a prominent Indian and sub-chief, who had been friendly with the colony at Manti, acted as interpreter, when a delegation of leading citizens went to the camp where a "peace pipe" was smoked and a "peace talk" held.

Later in the autumn a band of Indian musicians, accompanied by braves and squaws, visited the fort. Ammon was dressed in the fantastic garb of his tribe, which consisted of a fancy buckskin hunting shirt, trimmed with gay colored beads and long fringes of buckskin along the sleeves and around the waist. His leggings were also of buckskin, fringed up the sides and hung

EMELINE BIRD

with little bells, which jingled merrily to the graceful movements of the chief. Upon his head he wore a striking head dress of plumes, and buffalo horns protruded from either side of his head. The musicians had but one instrument, a tom-tom, made of green hide stretched over the end of a section of hollow tree, which being permitted to dry in the sun, made a very respectable drum. Upon this instrument several Indians beat time with wooden drum sticks. The singing was a kind of weird chant that rose and fell with a strikingly wild melody. The words they sang were: "Hi yah! hi yah; hi jay!" with a sharp explosive yell at intervals. The party went from door to door singing and dancing. The chief stood between two squaws while executing the dance, his bells making merry music. At intervals of perhaps a minute, the dancing and song would cease, and the chief would call out, "Sheteup, biscuit, shirt!" and the people would generously donate until a couple of sacks were filled with food stuffs. After the serenade the party returned to their wic!.-

i-ups and spent the eveningin feasting. As provisions were plentiful the whites gave to the Indians in abundance all kinds of produce and especially melons, of which they were as fond as a Tennessee darkey.

By such treatment the natives were retained in friendly relations with the whites although they gave them much trouble by turning their "pungoes." (ponies) into the gardens and fields. While the Indians would not herd their own ponies, they did not object seriously to the white papooses running the ponies off.

CHAPTER V.

LATE in the autumn war was very nearly precipitated by the accidental killing of an Indian near the lake border. In that day ducks and geese were plentiful and were much hunted by the whites as well as by the Indians. One day Riley Stewart was hunting and espying what he took to be a wolf, fired, and was horrified to find that he had killed an Indian. He immediately reported the matter to Captain Johnson, who called some of the people together and they went to the Indian camp, which was near by. James Mendenhall, who could converse in the Ute dialect, told the Indians what had happened. The redskins were much wrought up and it was only after a long parley that they were made to believe the killing accidental, and their friendship was retained by the payment of an ox and some powder and shot.

During the year 1851 Noah Packard and family came to Springville. also Edward O. Haymond and family. Mr. Haymond was the first blacksmith in Springville and for many years kept his anvil ringing. He also did the first gardening in the way of cultivating fruits and berries. Mr. Haymond was a very useful man in those early days, being always at the front in all public labors, which burdened the early settlers.

Edward Hall and family came early

NELSON D. CRANDALL

to Springville. Mr. Hall assisted James Potter and Jacob Houtz in building the first flouring mill in Springville, where O. M. Allen served as miller. This mill served the public for many years and made a good grade of flour. When the wheel and flume were ready for the water. nearly all the men and boys in town turned out with wagons, picks and shovels. built the dam and dug the race. their labor being paid for in mill work.

This year there were also added to the population of Springville the following: Thomas Guyman, L. G. Me calf, Ezra Parish and family, "Aunt" Betsy McBride and her four sons: Hyrum and Horace Clark; Enos, David, John and Simmons P. Curtis; Mormon and Moroni Miner and mother; Jabez and Nephi Durfee; Jerome Benson, H. H. Cole and family, Robert Johnson and family; John M. Stewart and family; Horace Wild and family; John, William and Robert McDonald; Elias Harmer and family; Wilbur Earl and family; James Oakly; and William and George Clyde, Albert Starr, and Luke William Gallup. Mr. Gallup was an adobe maker, and worked at the trade in the summer months and in the winters acted as village scribe, being able to write a good hand.

Large and abundant crops having been harvested this year, the winter of 1851-2 approached, without fear on the part of the settlers.

Miles Ingalls and Mrs. Phœbe Miller taught school during the autumn and winter in the fort schoolhouse, where the various gatherings for public worship, literary pursuits and dancing were held. Christmas and the New Year were celebrated with feasting, visiting and social amusements. The few books in the fort were read and re-read, as reading matter was very scarce in those days.

The mail was received from the East but twice a year and was eagerly looked for, because often an occasional letter and a few newspapers brought news from the childhood homes of our Springville pioneers.

Early in the winter of 1851-2 some surveying had been done by Andrew J. Stewart, including Plat A of our present city. In order that all might have a fair show in the selection of a city lot, after selecting the central location for the city public square and central school, the home lots were chosen by casting lots, all areas being numbered from one upward, written on slips of paper, shaken up in a box and drawn out. The lots were 12½ rods square.

Bishop Johnson's prize was the lot where now stand the residences of Hugh M. Dougall and Don C. Johnson. William Miller drew the lot where the tithing office now is; and Myron Crandall's, Richard Bird's and Cyrus Sanford's lots fell where portions of their families now reside.

Twenty acres of land was the maximum amount that each could claim for irrigation.

The first wells were dug in the spring of 1852. The first one is still supplying water upon the tithing house lot and was dug by William Miller.

This same spring a saw mill was completed at the mouth of Hobble creek canyon by H. H. Kearns and H. H. Cole. The settlers were now able to procure plenty of lumber from cedar, fir and pine logs hauled from the forks, and a building boom struck the town in good earnest.

On the 19th of April, 1852, the court met at Provo and Lucius N. Scoville was appointed clerk. The first business of the court was to levy a tax on all property for road purposes. The

AMOS S. WARREN

price of wheat was fixed at $1.50 per bushel for payment of said tax, and Springville was named as District No. 6. Ira Allen was appointed as road supervisor for the Springville district and Joseph Kelly was appointed as one of the examiners for the common schools. The judges of the school election to be held at the school house were William Miller and Myron Crandall.

Never, perhaps, in the history of our town has there been more bustle and life than during the season opening in the spring of 1852. Every family needed a home. A larger acreage was planted this season than ever before, and larger dams and canals were built. There was no difficulty in those days to get twenty men with plows and oxen to turn out and make a canal through the hard, baked soil. It was an animated scene when they began a canal. Ten oxen were attached to the largest plow in town, one fitted on purpose at "Pap" Haymond's forge. The most stalwart men were selected to hold the plow, one to wield the lash and steer the animals, while the remainder followed up, and with spade and shovel cleared away the loose earth. It is hinted that an occasional swear word was heard when the huge plow came in contact with a stump or stone and when the handles punched the plowmen in the ribs, or bucked at some obstruction and threw the unsuspecting riders off.

After the planting was done, logs began to come in to the saw mill. Before our saw mill was built all the logs used here were hauled to the mill at Provo. The first lumber used in the construction of the fort was cut there. It is said that the first load of logs taken from our canyon to Provo was hauled by William Smith and Sylvanus Hulett.

An adobe yard was laid off in the eastern part of Bishop Johnson's field, near which flowed, from beneath the bluff, the clear and cool "adobe yard spring," where often the laborer sat at noontide in the shade to eat his bread, which often had no other dressing than a dip in the sparkling water.

William Miller built the first adobe house outside the fort, the present tithing office. Aaron Johnson also built a larger adobe house, which all the old settlers will remember. This house, in its associations, became quite historic, because it was the only place for several years that was large enough for meetings, dances and public gatherings. It was here that the teachers held their deliberations; that the choir practiced; that the band met to practice and most of the business meetings were held. It was two stories high and contained twelve rooms. The three lower rooms were very large and were connected by folding doors, with large fire places in each end. Myron Crandall, Richard Bird and several others built adobe houses that year and many built of logs, while others moved their rooms from the fort onto their city lots.

Abram Day was the first adobe layer in Springville. He laid the adobes for Bishop Johnson's house, and Thomas Tew was the tender. It was upon this house that Mr. Tew took his first lessons in the trade which he has followed for the last forty-eight years. The lumber for these houses was made from logs taken out of Hobble creek canyon; the lath was made by cutting strips from $\frac{3}{8}$-inch cottonwood boards. The shingles were shaved with the draw knife on an old fashioned shaving horse. Many of the floors were pegged down on account of the scarcity of nails and their high price. The nails made by the village blacksmith were worth one cent each, for common eight penny or horse shoe nails, and passed current at that price.

By the time the storm clouds began to gather and the wintry blasts howl through the valley, ushering in the winter of 1853, our village had on quite an air of respectability.

During the autumn a number of immigrants had rolled through Main street in their prairie schooners, followed by their flocks, to settle farther south in the valley, so that the main street of our village had the appearance of much travel.

Many families had stopped here to cast their lot with the first comers, among whom can be remembered— Lorenzo Johnson, Huntington Johnson, the three Yager brothers, Murdock McKenzie, Walter Bird, Henry Brooks, Gardiner Curtis and family; John, Samuel and Lucy Pine; Jerome and Olive Benson; Laban Morril, George Mason, Joseph Kelly, Ransom Potter and family, Daniel Sumsion and family, Andrew Hamilton and family, John Maycock, Andrew Leslie, Newman Buckley and family, Elam Cheeney, Stephen Thornton, Horace Thornton, Joseph Bartholomew and family, William Robinson and family, William Bramall and family, Davis Clark, John Alleman and family, Cornelius Van-Leuvan, John Whitbeck and family, Aseph Blanchard and family, William Mendenhall and family, Sanford Fuller, Aaron Whittemore, and Mrs. Lucretia Warthen and family.

During the winter Bishop Johnson told the boys that if they would furnish fuel and lights, his large front rooms could be used for dancing. With the unanimity that usually exists with pioneer folk, all agreed to turn out and haul wood for a week.

Toward Christmas much snow had fallen and the lake was frozen over. Some bob sleds were hastily constructed and a party of ten or fifteen teams, headed by Bishop Johnson, went over the lake, remaining over night, and returning the next day, they brought two cords to the load of dry cedar wood. These trips were continued through the winter. The wood not only warmed but lighted the dwellings in those early days, as candles were very scarce. A very common light in those days, consisted of grease placed in a saucer, into which a wick, made of twisted cotton cloth, was laid. As the wick was burned it was clipped off with snuffers until all was consumed.

Levi Curtis secured the "assembly rooms" for cotillion parties, which were held weekly during the winter. Levi Curtis and James O'Banion were the fiddlers. Old and young would gather for dancing; everybody came early and returned about the midnight hour. The bed rooms opening from the hall were generally full of babies, snugly tucked away, while the mothers enjoyed the dance. Often supper was served in the spacious dining hall, attached to the Johnson home. Everything was done to make the gatherings delightful. These parties were pleasant and animated spectacles. The huge fire places at either end of the hall were piled high with dry cedar fagots, the flames from which, seemingly endowed with the spirit of the dance, leaped and danced up the chimneys with a roar that laughed the winter blasts to scorn. Candles held in place by three nails driven into wooden brackets, were ranged high along the walls, "And shed their soft lustre, and tallow on head dress and shawl," as Bret Harte says. Enough admission was charged to defray the expense of music and lights. Tickets were paid for in any kind of produce that the fiddlers could be induced to take. Usually a couple of two bushel sacks could be seen sitting near the door, into which the dancers deposited their contributions, and some brought candles with which to light up. The man with the candle commanded entrance to any of the social functions, no matter how swell the event, and it is even whispered that two have been admitted with one candle.

The New Year of 1853 was danced in with extra ceremony; more candles were furnished and another fiddler. William Smith, procured. All the good clothes were brought out for the occasion. Some who were mere lads at that time, wearing their first breeches, can remember among the merry makers, who were full of frolic and sprightly papers, William Miller, Cyrus Sanford and Gideon Wood of the middle aged, while the younger ones Milan Packard, William Roylance and Greg Metcalf cut the "pigeon's wing" and did the fancy steps. George McKenzie bowed and smiled at his fair partner and Procter Humphrey "swung 'em" because he "liked 'em." Those remembered by a boy, then five years old, as reigning belles are: Rebecca Parish, Olive Packard, Jane Haymond, Belle McKenzie and Sally Curtis. The old ladies sat and looked on, nodding their approval, while the old gentlemen sat in the chimney corners and told stories of the days when they were young.

This winter the school was taught by Mesdames Emeline and Phœbe Miller. Several concerts were given by local and Salt Lake City talent. The event of the season was the coming to Springville of a good orchestra from Salt Lake City, the members of which were: William C. Dunbar with his bag pipe, Henry Maiben, Henry E. Bowring, Phillip Margetts and Robert Neslin. They gave a series of musicales which were the town's topic for many days. The same orchestra came down again in the winter of 1853-4 and gave concerts in the "little school house" after its completion. In the winter of 1853 a brass band was organized by William D. Huntington, who held the position of bandmaster. The members of the band, so far as can be remembered were: Richard and William Bird, John W. Deal, Robert Johnson, Henry Roylance, Thomas Snelson, George and William Clyde, the latter playing the bass drum.

CHAPTER VI.

THE year 1853 marked an epoch in our village. The Legislative assembly of 1852 approved the city charter of Springville, Feb. 13, 1852. It may be mentioned here, that Springville was named from the large spring that furnishes water to the Houtz mill pond.

On April 4, 1853, the people met and held their first municipal election, when the following officers were elected: Mayor, Gideon D. Wood; Aldermen, Myron N. Crandall, David A. Curtis, James Guyman and Abraham Day; Councilors, Aaron Johnson, Lorenzo Johnson, William Miller, William D. Huntington, Ira Allen, H. H. Kearns, Murdock McKenzie and Stephen C. Perry; Marshal, Cyrus Sanford. It will be seen from the above array of officers, that our fathers believed that in a multitude of councilors there was safety, and what the aldermen, who were also justices of the peace, lacked in legal lore they made up in numbers. However the history of the next two years shows that the aldermen had nothing to do but draw their salaries which were usually nothing.

Summer schools were taught by Mrs. Emeline Miller and "Aunt" Betsey McBride, where all boys and girls too young to help their parents went to school. This summer the very first Sabbath school was organized under the immediate direction of Cyrus Sanford, Ira Allen and William Mendenhall.

GIDEON D. WOOD

The most notable event of this year was the outbreak of the famous Walker War. which kept the settlers in Utah. Juab and Sanpete counties in constant fear and commotion for a year. Hitherto peace had been maintained by our generous treatment of the natives.

The Indians had been allowed to consume tithing melons. potatoes and other perishable stuff and had been given "biscuit and a-muck" by the settlers. Some of the more belligerent colonists were in favor of feeding the Lamanites powder and shot, and now an opportunity presented itself. This account of the immediate cause of the outbreak of hostilities was given by an eye witness.

Andrew Leslie and John Maycock were watering grain in James B. Porter's field one day. a short distance beyond Spring creek. when a large party of Indians. who had been down on Provo river. came along. One of the squaws stopped at James Ivie's cabin. near by. and was bartering fish for flour. This doctrine of "quid pro quo" was new and distasteful to her dusky mate: he wished her to beg. and not buy. and commenced to beat and kick

his wife unmercifully. whereupon Mr. Ivie. who tradition says would not turn aside to avoid a "set to." requested the Indian to desist and "puck-a-chee." The now thoroughly enraged redskin drew an arrow upon Ivie and was about to let fly. when Ivie sprang aside and jumped upon his assailant. wrested the arrow from him in a trice. and struck the fellow on the head with a gun. At this critical moment another warrior. attracted by the hostile demonstration. was caught in the act of drawing a bead upon Ivie. by Joseph Kelly. and in a struggle his weapon was taken from him and he was stretched alongside his companion. by a stinging blow upon the head. Then the squaw. whom the whites had been trying to defend. seized a bow and arrow from her unconscious spouse and tried to shoot Ivie. but he seized her. took the arrow away and thrust her out of the cabin. During the melee. Leslie and Maycock hurried to the scene of hostilities. When they arrived they found the squaw pouring water on the head of her lord. When the Indian was in a condition to ride. the cavalcade proceeded to the house of Bishop Johnson. where a number of the brethren had already gathered. having heard of the affray. The Indians demanded. as a balm for the wounded crown. an ox and a gun. The Bishop was in favor of acceding to their demands. but some of the more hot headed were for fight. and did not believe in paying for an Indian's broken head. The Indians saw that their request was to be refused. and suddenly. with a wild war-whoop. brandished their arms and spurred their ponies southward through town toward Payson canyon. By this time the whites began to think they had acted unwisely and William Smith. Ransom Potter and A. B. Wild were dispatched by Bishop Johnson to overtake the Indians and offer them anything in reason to appease their rage. They found the Indians encamped at the mouth of Payson canyon and in a frenzy of excitement. Just before reaching the hostile camp, Wild and Potter were left with the horses, and Smith, the interpreter, advanced toward the redmen, shouting peace talk and making pacific signs with his hands. When he reached the Indians the first sight that greeted his eyes was the wounded Indian lying on a skin. Smith spoke to him and partially turned him over, but the wounded man only groaned in agony. Some of the leading Indians were called into a council and Smith asked what it would take to keep peace. After much gesticulating and guttural ejaculations, which the peace man could not understand, they finally expressed a willingness to settle the matter upon the payment of one beef, one gun and a pair of blankets. The white agent agreed to this demand, and an Indian was dispatched to town for the property, in company of the white envoys. The beef was soon forthcoming, also a gun, but the blankets, owing to their scarcity, were hard to procure, and the Indian evidently unable to control his anger, finally put spurs to his horse and with a fearful yell rode madly toward the hostile camp.

The situation now assumed a more serious aspect, and it was considered expedient to send another envoy to treat with the enraged Indians. Accordingly Stephen C. Perry, James Guyman, Davis Clark and Greg Metcalf, the latter going as interpreter, were hastily mounted and dispatched to overtake the frenzied savage, and purchase peace at any price. At the mouth of Payson canyon they found a large band of Indians in a very excited condition. Several chiefs in war paint rode around them brandishing their weapons in a threatening manner. After a time the interpreter gained the attention of the blood-thirsty savages, and tried to explain that the Indian himself was to blame, and that the

"white chief" was willing to pay an ox for the Indian's broken "cocoanut," and a new rifle for the broken one, also a pair of blankets. But all terms were rejected. For a time things appeared hopeless for the white men, and it was only by the utmost persuasion on the part of the chiefs, that the envoys were permitted to return to the settlement.

At this time Walker was camped at Peteetneet (now Payson) with several hundred braves. During a lull in the excitement, just before the envoys started for home, they administered to the wounded Indian, who was in a serious condition. This seemed to inspire the Indians with awe; and the interpreter told them that if the brave died, the white men would pay "heap beef" for him. A few minutes after the departure of the white men, the Indian died.

It was just dark, and as soon as the envoys were well out of sight, they took a cut-off, known to one of the party, and thereby saved their lives; for no sooner had they gotten well on their way than the Indians, with a wild yell, started in pursuit, but taking the regular road they missed their opportunity for revenge. As soon as the Indian died pandemonium broke loose, the redskins being perfectly wild. Walker was greatly enraged, and that night he and some of his men rode into Payson and shot a man named Kiel, who was standing guard. The alarm was spread rapidly throughout the county, and companies of minute men were organized to rush to any point where their assistance might be most urgently needed.

On the morning following the killing of Kiel, a cavalry company was organized under the direction of General Johnson and sent to the front, arriving at Payson almost before the blood had cooled in the body of the dead man. The company was fully organized and in the saddle in two hours. There were

10 days of enlistment or medical examinations. but "Hurrah! boys. and off we go!" The captain of that company was Mathew W. Caldwell: first lieutenant. James Guyman: second lieutenant. Joseph Kite: orderly serjeant. Andrew B. Wild: and so far as can now be ascertained the names of other members were: Milan and Nephi Packard. Geo. B. Matson. Sanford Fuller. Geo. McKinzie. Asa Boice. Wm. D. Johnson. Proctor Humphrey. Myron Crandall. Wm. Smith and Nelson Spafford. As there was no appearance of Indians in the vicinity. the company. after reconnoitering the surrounding country. returned to Springville in the evening. On this night. July 19. while Lyman S. Wood and a squad of troopers were on picket guard out upon the edge of Union bench. near where Wm. Kerswell now lives. they were ambushed and Wm. Jolly was shot through the right arm. The alarm was spread and a relief party sent out in hot haste. who brought the wounded man in. while great excitement reigned at the fort. About July 23 ten men were called to go to the aid of the fort at Manti. with Captain Whipple's company from Provo. The members of that platoon so far as can be gathered were Lieut. Ben Richmond. Serjt. J. W. Bissell. Wm. Hatch. Amos Warren. Isaac Potter. Edw. Clyde and a couple of men by the names of Case and Neilson. They went with a little bread and onions in their haversacks as their only food.

During this war guards were posted and lookouts were kept from the tops of the highest houses. A smoke by day and a bright fire by night were the signals adopted to warn the people in the various settlements of the approach of the painted foe. and to call for help as the occasion might demand. Nelson Spafford. Cyrus Sanford and Joseph Kelly were very active as express riders during the continuance of this war. Nearly all the able bodied men

JOSEPH KELLY

and boys were enrolled in the minute companies. and were out on several expeditions.

As a measure of safety a new fort was constructed. surrounding four blocks. Block houses. in which the people lived during the hostilities. were built at intervals. The buildings were connected by a stockade ten feet high. which was built of logs set three feet deep in the earth. All the residents outside the fort row were called in. and a strong guard stationed outside every night for months. These were indeed dark and gloomy times for the beleagured people. as the hostiles were numerous while the white men were few. The herds went out upon the bottoms every day accompanied by a strong guard. and were corralled within the fort at night. A signal gun was to be fired from the lookout on the housetop if the Indians appeared. to warn the farmers and herdsmen to hasten to the shelter of the fort. The wildest rumors were afloat at times of massacres and threatened attacks by the savages. Several times during the summer and fall of 1853 word came that the fort was to be attacked by hundreds of the foe. Upon these several occasions the women and children were gathered into General Johnson's house, the guards were doubled and a picket guard put out to give the alarm in case the foe was found to be advancing.

One evening, in particular, is well remembered. It was early in the fall, and the harvests had been gathered within the defended circle. The alarm had spread that Walker, with a great number of warriors, would make an attack in the night, intending to massacre the inhabitants of the fort. There was no sleeping that anxious night by the vigilant adults, nor by the children who were mostly old enough to sense their danger. During the long night express riders dashed up, with dispatches from Provo and Spanish Fork. All would gather around the rider to hear the brief news, then an opening would be made in the crowd and the courier would speed away to the neighboring town to report that all was yet well. One of the best remembered

riders that night was Joseph Kelly. Once he spurred into town from Provo, reined his horse back upon its haunches, and after a hurried conversation with General Johnson dashed away toward Spanish Fork, returning in less than an hour to report all well there. Thus a chain of communication was formed by these men on their fleet horses from Lehi to Payson. The houses of Johnson and Miller, as well as the door yards, were crowded with women and children trying to sleep. Here you might have seen a mother trying to quiet the fears of her larger children, while yonder a young mother was singing a lullaby to a fretful babe. Old men and women sat silently in the corners, awaiting the warwhoop which they felt sure would come during the night. The only thing to vary the fearful monotony was the arrival of the express rider, or the relief of the guard. Thus the anxious hours dragged slowly along, and day broke upon the anxious inhabitants of the fort. No sign of Indian warriors had been seen, and as the sun mounted the heavens their courage returned. Much the same state of affairs continued during the autumn

BISHOP JOHNSON'S HOME.

and winter. From Aaron Johnson's journal it is learned that the trouble and expense were considerable. It is thus itemized: Services of men and supplies furnished. $2,000; building of stockade around four city blocks, $3,000. While the men were performing the necessary military duties, many of the women worked in the fields. There are many women, still living in our town, who were seen in those exciting times, working on the threshing floor, while their fathers and brothers were upon scouting expeditions.

In the spring of 1854 peace was declared with Walker.

Early in the spring, while William Smith and Thomas Sprague were doing picket duty on the East bench, they discovered, near the Oak springs, a band of Indians, who did not seem to be in hostile array. The whites rode across the creek toward the redmen, making peace signs, which were returned by the natives. Hereupon Smith left his gun and horse with his companion and walked over to the Indians, where he found Sow-i-ett and White Eye, sub-chiefs whom he knew. They said they were tired of war and wanted peace. Smith replied in the same strain, and invited them to go with him to see Bishop Johnson, which after many assurances of fair treatment upon the part of Smith, they consented to do. Three of them came to town and saw the "white chief," had a long talk and a good dinner. They were given an invitation for "all hands" to come down next day for a big smoke and a fine dinner.

The next morning forty warriors presented themselves at the Johnson home, where they were seated at a big table in the large rooms, with the Bishop and Smith seated with them. They were feasted to a surfeit with "succotash" and other dishes so relished by the native and sent away rejoicing. This was the first step to the peace that soon followed, as when

DAVIS CLARK

Walker came in the final pipe of peace was smoked and the hatchet buried deep, so far as Walker was concerned, for he was a staunch friend to the "white brothers" ever afterward.

Brigham Young, with a party, came to Springville in the winter of 1853 and held a series of meetings. While here he visited the site of the proposed new school house, and remarked that he would like to hitch his mules to it and pull it larger each way. Consequently it was concluded to build a larger wing on the south-east corner of the "big school house" and the foundation was partly laid, but was never finished.

Lyman Wood taught the first school in the "little schoolhouse." The names of those who taught school in this house, and under whom the author received instruction in the rudiments of an education, where the birch switch was a lively factor, were, Walter Savage, A. F. McDonald, Wilbur Earl, Charles D. Evans and Emerson C. Felton, a young teacher from the East.

In the autumn a sad accident cast a gloom over the spirits of the settlers. As parties were returning from the canyon with timber for the stockade. Orrin Packard was thrown from his wagon, and run over by the heavy load. He was taken up by tender hands and carried to his home, where he died in a few hours. The accident occurred on "Packard's dugway," four miles east of town in Hobble creek canyon, and has since been called by that name.

So far as can be learned, there came to Springville to live in 1853, Phillip, Richards, David and Joseph M. Westwood; Phillip Hurst, Joseph W. Bissel, Loren Roundy, Sipriam Marsh, one of our first shoemakers: Jordan Davis with his widowed mother and brothers, George, Robert, Charles, Joseph and Orson; Thomas and J. H. Noakes.

This winter the laws of consecration were taught to a considerable extent and the people were called upon to "consecrate their property to God," which most of them did. The author was shown one of those old consecration papers, by James Oakley, who was one to obey the call. It is certified to by Lucien N. Scoville as clerk, and contains an invoice of the property thus turned over. It is important here to state that none of the property ever left the hands of the donors, but it proved the people's willingness, at that time, to obey the command of the priesthood.

CHAPTER VII.

IN the spring of 1854 the settlers undertook another stupendous job, that of building a mud wall around the city plat, three-fourths of a mile square, as an additional protection against Indians. This wall was eight feet wide at the base, four feet thick at the top and twelve feet high. It was made out of the earth in line of the wall, and on the outer streets of the city, which were eight rods wide. Two rods were used for the wall and moat on the outside. This wall was built by first constructing a frame work with caps on the top. Planks were placed within the rows of timbers to hold the soil until dry. There were three gang of men and a general boss of construction. One party set the posts in line and put the planks in place; one shoveled in the earth, and the third, with heavy pounders, settled the earth down solidly. Several sections of the wall would be under construction at the same time, and as fast as they were finished, the planks and posts were moved forward. Heavy gates were made at the four sides, at the terminations of Main and Center streets, with bastions and port holes

EMMA SPAFFORD

on each side. There were bastions at the corners of the town for enfilading the walls if necessary.

A public tax was levied for the purposes of construction. The wall was almost completed by New Year's day. 1855. The wall extended from where E. P. Brinton's house now stands. around the city to Center street on the west. The vacancy was so remote from the canyons that it was thought there could be no danger of an attack on that side.

On New Year's day a grand celebration was held in commemoration of the finishing of the wall.

It had been an open winter and there was no snow on the ground: the sun shone warmly and everything was propitious for an out door celebration.

A procession was formed. with banners bearing mottoes flying to the wind. The brass band. lead by John Taylor. headed the procession. The line of march was from the public square north on Main street to the north gate of the city. where an incline had been arranged. up which the procession marched two by two, to the top of the wall. thence along the top to the north-east corner of the city. Here the procession descended to the street and formed a hollow square. where speeches. toasts and music whiled the happy hours away. Then the procession was again formed and marched to the public square and dismissed.

In the autumn of 1854 William D. Huntington. William Smith. L. G. Metcalf. Jackson Stewart. James Mendenhall and John Whitbeck were called to go to the Elk mountains. Arizona. to look for a place or places for colonization. There were others from the North. making a large company under the guidance of "High Forehead." a local Indian chief. While upon this trip they discovered some of the wonderful dwellings and fortifications of the Cliff Dwellers. One stone house which they explored was situated under a shelving cliff. well built and containing twenty-five rooms. The party returned about Christmas without finding a desirable location. While upon their journey they were many times compelled to take their wagons apart and lift them piece by piece up the perpendicular sides of the cliffs. leading their animals by circuitous and dangerous paths to the heights above. until the wagons could be taken no farther. when they were abandoned and never recovered.

This winter the meetings were held. and dances also. in the Johnson home. During the winter the first drama was put on the boards in the "little school house." The title of the play was. "The Maid of Croisy." with the following cast of characters: Sergeant Austerlitz. Wilbur Earl: Captain Francis. Lyman S. Wood: Walter. Phillip Westwood: Theresa. Miss Electa Wood: Nannette. Mrs. Phillip Westwood. The performance concluded with the farce. "Perfection." with members of the

NELSON SPAFFORD

above east, with Miss Belle McKenzie playing the lead and Miss Temperance Westwood playing the soubrette. That first dramatic entertainment was much enjoyed.

This same winter a singing class was organized by a Mr. Messenger, from the East, and nearly all the people in town, young and old, turned out to be instructed. Aaron Johnson was the chief patron, having taken tuition to the value of a beef ox, and sent ten members of his family, as well as his two hired men. Great enthusiasm reigned and everybody sang.

Edwin Lee and George B. Matson cast their lot with the Springville people this year, and both have been active participants in all the work of subduing the wilderness.

Debates were held weekly through the winter of 1854-5, where practical and occult subjects were discussed by the debaters of the village. Prominent among those who took part in the controversies were William Miller, A. F. McDonald, Asael Perry, John M. Stewart, Aaron Johnson, Noah Packard and Wilbur Earl.

Spelling schools were popular this winter also. The class was arranged on each side of the house, under the leaders, who chose them, and the preceptor would give out the words beginning at the head, alternating from one side to the other, down the line to the foot until all were spelled down. Webster's blue backed speller was the book used.

The band that had been instructed the previous winter by John Taylor, a musician from Provo, gave several concerts, which were greatly enjoyed. The members of that band had belonged to good organizations in the old country and had brought their instruments with them; therefore they were able to give a musical entertainment of a high order. The members of the band, the previous winter, paid John Taylor $40 per month to come from Provo and give them two lessons a week. Afterward Mr. Taylor came here to live and the band under his instruction made rapid progress. The members of the second brass band were John Taylor, William D. Huntington, William C. Huntington, Robert Johnson, Henry Roylance, Thomas Snelson, George and William Clyde, and two others, whose names cannot now be recalled.

Early in the winter a variety performance was given as a public benefit, in which the local talent was represented. One number that will be remembered by the old settlers, was a dialogue entitled, "Joseph Smith and the Devil," which was published about that time in the Millennial Star, and was very popular. William Miller impersonated Joseph Smith, and A. F. McDonald his satanic majesty. Miller was dressed in the conventional high hat and swallow tail coat, and McDonald wore the traditional caudal appendage protruding between the swallow tails of his coat. James M. Pierce represented the famous Paganini, with cornstalk fiddle accompaniment, much

WILLIAM J. STEWART

MILAN PACKARD

to the amusement of the younger portion of the audience.

In the summer of 1854 the first ditch was made from Hobble creek upon the Union bench and farms were taken up and worked for a few years, and· were then abandoned in consequence of the scarcity of water. At this period the Union bench was covered with luxuriant bunch grass upon which the cattle would soon fatten, and caused the cows to give the riches milk in abundance.

During the year Aaron and Lorenzo Johnson were the United States mail contractors, carrying the mail from Salt Lake City to Nephi. At one time in the month of June there was great difficulty in crossing the Provo river, in consequence of the high water.

Mrs. Jane Johnson had gone to Salt Lake on a visit, and upon her return the river was so high that the mail carrier refused to take his only passenger over the dangerous and rushing torrent. The mail passed over in safety, however, while the homesick lady was left with a family in a cabin on the other side, to await the assuag-

ing of the water. Some days later the coach made its return trip and took another passenger, who now bears the name of Hannah Huntington. Bishop Johnson took old Jack and Bay and a light wagon, and went along to see the coach safely over the flood and also to bring back his wife. When they came to the river's brink, there was no diminution of the flood. The large horses were placed beside the coach horses on the upper side, the Bishop riding the up-stream animal, when all plunged in four abreast and made the passage in safety, though not without great peril. Mrs. Johnson, now thoroughly homesick, would rather risk crossing the angry stream than to remain any longer in her isolated quarters, so she was placed on old Jack's back, and with a firm grip on the surcingle was ready for the crossing. Her companion mounted the larger animal, and taking a firm hold of the halter of the other they entered the stream. Several times the strong horses

JANE PACKARD

were swept from their feet and the riders thought they would have to go down, but after a hard struggle they emerged on the other side in safety.

In the summer of this year the equanimity of the village was somewhat disturbed by the death of Squash-Head, an Indian who for years had been the terror of the neighborhood. He was charged, among other savage atrocities, with having killed and eaten a two-year-old white child, on the other side of the lake. He had many times threatened to kill certain citizens, unless blankets and other things were forthcoming. Squash-Head levied this tribute because his brother had died in his absence, and the white men had buried the corpse without the usual accompaniment of arrows, tomahawks, horse and blanket which were supposed to assist him in reaching the "Happy Hunting Grounds." His threats caused a posse to be sent out to effect his capture. He was surprised and arrested in the Tintic region, and brought to Springville where he was detained a couple of days before being taken to Salt Lake City for trial.

The posse encamped in Bishop Johnson's enclosure, where their meals were supplied by the Bishop's family. The front room was used as a kind of a military prison, while the men stood guard outside. Squash-Head—whose name was very appropriate as he had a very large head, round as a squash, and adorned by a huge mouth in which gleamed a set of teeth a chimpanzee might have been proud of—was ironed with a ball and chain upon his ankles and wrists. On the second morning of his detention, while the guards were eating breakfast preparatory to starting for the capital with their prisoner, old Squash-Head settled his case by severing his jugular vein with a sharp bread knife which had been given him with his breakfast. He fell forward upon the hearth, his chains clanking so loudly as to attract the attention of his solitary guard, who was standing near by. It was darkly hinted at the time that some white person had done the bloody deed, but every indication pointed to the fact that the Indian, who feared hanging as a just punishment for his crimes, had been the means of his own taking off. The wrath of the other Indians was cooled down by supplying them liberally with melons, potatoes and other edibles. As a matter of fact, they were glad to be rid of him, as he was feared by the entire band.

CHAPTER VIII.

ON the 4th of April, 1855, after a stirring canvass, the following officers were elected to look after the civil interests of the city for the ensuing two years: Mayor, William Miller: Aldermen, Noah Packard, Myron N. Crandall, Abram Day, Orrin Craw: Councilors, Stephen Perry, David A. Curtis, Philander J. Perry, Aaron Johnson, Gideon D. Wood, Ezra Parrish, William Huggins, M. Curtis, Smith Humphrey: Recorder, John M. Stewart: Marshal, Cyrus Sanford, 1855.

By this time there was a home on nearly every lot in Plat A, and most of the lots had been fenced. The old-fashioned ditch-fence was much in evidence. It consisted of a ditch two feet wide at the bottom, three feet deep and three feet wide on top, the earth all being piled in an even hillock along the inside bank and surmounted

"Ten thousand bushels, with might and main,
Have we reaped of the golden grain."

HARVEST SCENE AT MAPLETON.   ETHER BLANCHARD IN THE FOREGROUND.

by a pole fence. This season in May the creek showed a rising spirit. For the first time the narrow channel was full and foaming, and at some places over-running its banks. It then ran in its natural channel, crossing State street where it now does, then turning a square corner ran north just in front of the Dinwoodey building to the point where the old cottonwood tree stands; then turned west. The channel was about sixteen feet wide and of a uniform depth of seven feet. The bridge was washed away and for some time the stream was impassable, except at a point on East street. Two heavy poles were thrown across the stream on Main street and lashed together, as a footbridge. An accident occurred here before the hand-railing was completed, whereby one of the children of the village was drowned "stone dead" for a short time. Merrill Lane, a nephew of Bishop Johnson, started after the cows one evening, and was compelled to cross on the poles. Aaron Johnson, a child of five years, wanted to cross, so Lane took the little fellow upon his back and started across. The swift waters rocked the bridge and the foam dashed into the air. When the boys reached the middle of the bridge Lane lost his head—also his foot-hold—and fell into the boiling flood! He caught the poles and held on like grim death, while the little fellow went under the bridge in the midst of the foaming, whirling water, like a chip upon its bosom. One of his brothers ran along the bank and howled for help. James Sylvester, who was working at his forge near by, ran to the rescue. He caught a firm hold on some willows growing on the bank and leaped into the stream neck-deep, caught the almost drowning boy and landed him before life was quite extinct.

About mid-summer a band of Indians pitched their wick-i-ups in Bishop Johnson's pasture. There were some thirty families with their chief. This chief had recently married a young squaw, and had constructed for her a bowery near the head of the mill pond. After a few days the chief was taken violently ill and died. The herd-boys. whose duties called them near the camp, saw the excitement. Every squaw in camp began to howl in a manner that would have put a band of coyotes to shame. In order that their spirits might help their chief past the Devil, and accompany him to the place of the Great Spirit, two horses and five favorite dogs were slain. A rifle shot from the region of the bride's bower caused the herd-boys to run to the spot where they were shocked to see the bride of a week lying in a pool of blood, dead. The murderer had skulked behind the high willows, and taking aim had shot her in the head. All the bows and arrows were broken up, and just at sunset the camp was pulled up and the cortege wended its way, chanting dolefully, up to the mouth of Hobble creek canyon, where they buried the chief with his gun and knives beside him. The squaw, horses and dogs were left where they fell, and the owner of the field was compelled to send his hired men to bury them.

In 1855 the Spanish Fork, Provo and Springville boys were engaged in hostilities. With the Provo boys the feelings became so bitter and the encounters so frequent that the bishops and teachers had to interfere. The boys of the three rival villages were known among themselves as the "Springville Sharpers," the "Provo Pacers" and the "Spanish Fork Gophers." When a band of our herd-boys met a band of "Gophers" out in the clay-beds an encounter was sure to

ensue, in which slings, switches and mud-throwers were called into requisition. These mud-throwers were the herd-boys' ideal weapons. It was a hickory switch, six feet long, with a ball of clay pressed upon the end. This missile was projected into space by a dextrous turn of the wrist, and sent flying to its mark with great precision and velocity, and wherever it struck the body a large and painful welt was raised. Scarcely a day passed without a collision between the "Sharpers" and "Gophers," from which no particular harm came. But not so when the "Sharpers" met the "Pacers" on the other side of town. Spring creek, which marked the boundry of the rival villages, contained the three swimming holes, which were claimed as the property of each. The rivals would often meet peaceably and compare their skill in swimming; but often some dispute would arise and an encounter was the inevitable result, in which all sorts of weapons were used, teeth, fists, stones, clubs and mud-throwers. Sometimes the "Pacers" would put to flight the "Sharpers, and sometimes the "Sharpers" were victorious. One day a number of young men came from Provo to help their little brothers, and it so happened that the "Sharpers" had brought their big brothers with them. A quarrel was easily provoked and a general engagement took place, which resulted in a decisive victory for the "Sharpers." Two of the larger Provo boys were shamefully beaten, and had to be helped home by their comrades. After the fight our boys broke up a plow that lay in a field on the Provo side and threw the pieces into the stream. Charges were made by some Provo parties against Springville's belligerents, for bodily injuries done, also for the destruction of the plow. The "Sharpers" were fined fifty cents each to pay for the plow and the broken heads. Bad feelings continued between the rival factions for several years.

This was the year of the famous "grasshopper war," which was more disastrous in its results than the Indian trouble had been. The pests had come in the autumn of 1854 in such myriads, as to darken the sun at noonday, and deposited their eggs everywhere; they hatched out next summer and swept almost everything before them.

The usual crops were growing nicely, when the grasshoppers began to move upon the young grain. Ditches were plowed, into which water was run, but it proved no impediment to the foragers. Winrows of straw were put down and when blackened with the insects, were burned, but there was no apparent diminution in their numbers, and many gave up in despair. About the time the wheat was in the head the destroying hordes commenced to fly and attack the more remote fields. Now the struggle began in earnest. Men, women and children turned out, with brush in hand, and marched through the standing grain, applying the brush vigorously, causing the pest to fly upward in such clouds as to

obscure the sun; and by arduous labor of weeks duration, about one-fourth of the crops were saved.

One amusing incident is remembered and is worth relating: The flying hoppers seldom commenced to breakfast where they rested over night. Richard Bird had two acres of beautiful wheat north of town, nearly ripe. He had placed a winrow of straw around the field, in order to burn the pests if they made an invasion. Sure enough a cloud of them came one evening about sundown and settled comfortably upon the straw for the night. Richard thought his time for revenge had come, he applied a match to the straw, which flashed up like tinder, only burning their wings off and then going out, leaving the voracious intruders otherwise robust and hearty. Being unable to fly they remained and finished the crop for breakfast. In the autumn the mauraders deposited their eggs for another year, but shortly afterward there came a warm spell, which hatched out the eggs then and there, so the crops the next year were not harmed.

In consequence of a scarcity of water a large field of wheat on Dry creek was about to burn up. Bishop Johnson called for all the able bodied men in the village to turn out, with teams and shovels, to dig a canal that would supply water for the perishing crop. Every man responded and worked with a will. A canal was dug from the Houtz mill pond to Dry creek, 3½ miles long, 6 feet wide and 18 inches deep, with water running through it in four days. The wheat was saved and a good crop secured, it having escaped the ravages of the "Ironclads," as the grasshoppers were called.

On the 4th of July it was agreed that all should turn out, with teams, picks and a boss, and haul the foundation rock for the big school house which the fathers had concluded to build. It was to be used as a church

EDWIN LEE

also until one could be built. When first constructed it was two stories high, and a large belfry graced the front gable. On the 24th the men went up the canyon and quarried the stone, just above the locality known now as the Second Bridge. At noon they returned and partook of a public dinner, under the bowery, prepared by the women of the village. 1855

In the fall of this year, Abram Day, William Miller and Aaron Johnson completed an adobe flouring mill, just east of the Latter Day Saints meeting house. George Storrs, who came to Springville this autumn, was the miller, with John Angus as assistant.

Those who came to Springville to live this year, so far as can be recalled are: Robert Watson, one of our early carpenters; James Stevenson, the first tailor; H. M. Dougall, his brother William and their mother; William Bromley, Henry Clucas and family; and John Metcalf, a mechanic.

During the winter A. F. McDonald and Walter Savage taught school in the little school house, where the older pupils received advanced instruction, while minor schools were taught in other places.

One of the leading events of this winter was a school exhibition, given by the members of the McDonald-Sav-

age school. It was the very first of the kind ever given in our city, and was hailed with delight by everyone. Portions of the play of "William Tell," as it appeared in McGuffy's reader, were rendered, with Mr. Savage as William Tell, John S. Boyer as Albert, Murray Messenger as Sarnem, and the other Boyer boys and Sumner Messenger being conspicuous in the cast. The boy stood on the burning deck, David slew Goliah, and the doctor took the dose intended for his patient and altogether the entertainment was a roaring success.

It may be here mentioned that others of our early teachers were: Zebedee Warren, John S. Fullmer, Uriah E. Curtis, Oliver B. Huntington, Harriet Knight, Jane Johnson, Mrs. Singleton and Thomas B. Marsh. In relation to the latter gentleman, it will be remembered that he was one of the early apostles of the Latter Day Saints church, who apostatized and subsequently returned to the church. He came to Springville in 1857 and was employed, by Bishop Johnson, to teach a kind of kindergarten for the children of the neighborhood. The school was held on the Johnson lot beneath a shady bower, and the instruction was mostly oral.

CHAPTER IX.

THE spring of 1856, succeeding the "grasshopper war," was one of scarcity: many of our people never tasting bread for months. The writer of these lines can remember men now living, who came regularly to the pasture to dig thistle roots for food. Pig weeds and red root were used as greens and the sego bulb was much sought after. Those who had

raised wheat the previous year disposed of as much as they could spare to their luckless neighbors. Flour went up to $24 per hundred and was scarce even at that price. One instance will illustrate the liberality of Aaron Johnson, the father of the colony. Early in the spring he counted and rationed his family on one pound of flour per head, a day, until the 15th day of July. when the early harvest would be ready. He did not make any allowance for the transient traveller. who might come along. Be it remembered that there were no hotels in that early day and the bishop's home was the regular stopping place. He had his wheat ground and after deducting the rations for his own own family. old the remainder for $6 per hundred although speculators offered him $24 per hundred. Though there were several ruses were adopted by the speculators. to get some of the flour at $6 per hundred for speculative purposes. the bishop learned of and defeated the schemes. About July 1st his flour gave out. but some barley that had ripened was threshed out and used for making bread until the dry land wheat ripened and was threshed out and milled. when bread was again plentiful in the settlement.

Fine crops were raised and as the harvest was an early one. they had a celebration. a sort of Thanksgiving day. on the 24th of July. A bowery had been erected on the public square. all done in one day by the united efforts of the people. A splendid program was rendered in the forenoon. There were twenty-four young ladies in white and a like number of gentlemen in black. all carrying banners. The fathers and mothers in Israel. the "Silver Greys." and the Mexican war veterans. marched and counter marched on the public square. Lyman S. Wood led the young men and his sister. Electa Wood. led the young women. At 1 p. m. the banquet was spread in the bowery and all partook of the bounties of the fields and gardens. And such a feast it 'was!' After the long time of fasting and almost starvation. it was truly appreciated. One feature of the feast was a barbecue. An ox had been roasted whole. together with several young porkers: while fowl of every kind filled out the bill of fare. and the tables groaned beneath their

loads. After the settlers had regaled the inner man. a band of some fifty Indians were permitted to clean up the wreck. which they did to a nicety.

One incident of the feast worthy of mention is remembered: After all were seated and the chaplain was mouthing rather a long prayer. old "Doctor Indian" stepped up to the edge of the bowery. where two boys were standing. and asked them what the man was saying. On being informed that he was telling God how thankful they were for the food. the medicine man ejaculated. "Ugh! God no sabie white man talk. He sabie Injun talk. me tell Him in Injun." Whether he ever told Him or not in Injun was never found out: however. the medicine man was filled up on the fragments of the feast.

In the afternoon everyone danced on the ground under the bowery. where the surface was packed down hard. Thus sped the merry hours to the strains of sweet music and the tripping of nimble feet. The evening hours were passed in witnessing a dramatic performance. given under the bowery. by the home dramatic company. A stage had been built with the sides and back concealed with wagon covers. The curtain was also a large wagon cover. A board in front of the curtain. with inch holes bored at intervals held the candles for the footlights. It was a beautiful moonlight night and the audience gathered early to listen to the orchestra. The name of the play has been forgotten and the only members of the cast who can be recalled are: A. F. McDonald. Wilbur Earl. Nephi Packard and Mary Jane Matson. There was a soldier and a sailor: a villian and a funny man: a sighing lover and a love-lorn damsel.

During the autumn the work on the big school house progressed. L. W. Gallup. the chief adobe maker. with a contingent of mixers and moulders. prepared the material for the walls.

THE LATTER DAY SAINTS' MEETING HOUSE, BUILT IN 1856.

The logs from which the lumber was made came from the "Big Slide," were cut by Thomas Sprague, Abram Noe, Newman Bulkley and others, run down on the snow as far as it lasted, and then snaked to the skidway near the Oak Springs. One Sunday a noon after meeting Bishop Johnson as all the male members to remain to a ass meeting. It was customary then to take Sunday afternoon in which to plan for all public enterprises for the coming week. At this meeting the Bishop called for thirty teams to volunteer to go after the logs that had been cut for the building, then in course of erection. The teams were soon forthcoming, and they planned to meet at the eastern gate at sunrise the next morning, and proceed to the canyon together. At the appointed time the thirty teams were ready and rolled out together to the mountains. When the skidway was reached, all unhitched and, loading the chains upon the yokes of the oxen, they went up to the big log-pile. The logs were usually cut in the winter when the snow had hardened sufficiently to permit running them down. The logs when peeled, and sharpened upon one end, would fly down the mountain like a shot from a gun. Sometimes in turning a curve in the canyon the log would shoot into the air, and, coming down on its point bury itself so deeply in the ground that it was only dug out with much labor. A flying log would sometimes strike one of these standing logs and split it asunder. It was wild and dangerous sport.

It was quite dark before the wagons were loaded. They drove down and unloaded at the mill at the mouth of the canyon, and returned home about 11 o'clock after a most tiresome but profitable day. Bishop Johnson's memoirs declare that the log he delivered that day was a white pine 3½ feet in diameter at the top, 18 feet long, and made 900 feet of inch lumber.

Thus the good work progressed. The

WILLIAM WORDSWORTH

feet of its surface in 1856. A mass meeting was called to get teams to go to the canyon for the wood out of which the corral was to be built. They met at the eastern gate and proceeded up toward the canyon. As they approached the dugway at the mouth of the canyon. they saw a huge grizzly bear. feasting upon the "servis" berries which hung in great profusion on the bushes. The brute was standing on his hind legs. and with his 4-inch claws pulled the branches down so he could chew off the fruit. A council of war was held. and it was discovered that there was not a weapon in the company adequate to put the quietus upon the animal. Bishop Johnson had that morning purchased a Colt's revolver from William Warren. and there were several small rifles in the crowd: it was hastily concluded to dispatch a man upon a fleet horse to town for a Yager—at that time one of the most effective guns in use. Andrew Wild was the owner of the gun: Milan Packard volunteered to go after it. and old Jack. of the Johnson team. was selected for the race. Just

scaffolding was alive with masons and tenders. and the material was quickly passed from scaffold to scaffold. Some of those who were active in the construction and are still living are James Oakley. Thomas Tew. William Mendenhall and George B. Matson. who had learned the mason's trade in Deleware: Joseph Kelly and Robert Watson were the chief mechanics.

In this autumn another incident of a public nature occurred—the building of a public corral. in which the stock could be gathered at the semi-annual "round-ups" held every spring and autumn. and which were looked forward to by the village boy as a time when he could mount his pony. and with whip and spur and dog along-side dash over the range like a wild Apache to gather the herds for identification and branding. This corral was situated just north of the north-east corner of the public square. upon a lot that had been set apart for the purpose. That space was afterward pre-empted by the creek. which washed away six

JOHN BOYLANCE

after the rider had dashed away, old bruin, having satisfied his hunger, went down to the little marsh at the foot of the dugway and stretched himself, with a grunt of satisfaction, among the cool grasses, all unconscious of the presence of the men and his own impending doom. The horses were unhitched and kept ready to mount in case the enemy, when aroused, might attack them. Thus matters hung in suspense for a quarter of an hour, when Johnson, giving the reins of his horse to one of the party, approached quietly to within twenty feet of the now sleeping animal. Not a movement was discerned and the hunter decided to take a shot, which he did. Still the animal remained quiet, and they decided the shot had killed him or missed the mark entirely. They, therefore, awaited the return of Packard, who soon came in sight, his horse all flecked with foam. A cool man was given the Yager for the final attack, while all stood ready at the bridle to mount and keep out of the way of the animal in case he should only be wounded. The marksman approached the huge animal, which had not been seen to move a hair since lying down. A sure aim was taken; leaden missile went to the mark and the grizzly was the second 'time shot. The pelt was removed and given to the Bishop for having fired the first shot, and the meat was divided among the men, while the claws were carried away as a trophy by Andrew Wild, and mounted upon the harnesses of his horses. The skin was tanned and served the Johnson boys as a bed for many years on their canyon trips.

CHAPTER X.

IN the autumn of 1856, before the big school house was plastered, our first city fair was held. There had been a county fair at Provo and the settlers at Springville decided to see what could be done along that line in their own town. There was a fine display of fruits; corn that stood eight feet high; wheat six feet high, with heads six inches long; potatoes large enough to fill a pot and melons upon which ten men could regale themselves and have melon left. No tame fruit had yet been raised. There were specimens of homespun knitted goods, linen, etc., which showed that the mothers and daughters had not been idle. Wild flowers adorned the building, and a few pictures which had been sacredly kept as momentoes of the old homes, were hung. There were old books wherein an "s" was fashioned like an "f", and quaint old slippers of our grandmothers' day; a few dolls, relics of our mothers' childhood days, gazed upon the audience with their beady eyes and caused the little girls to clap their tiny hands with joy. A hobby horse, with saddle and trappings, fashioned by the village genius, George Roberts, held the future rough riders in speechless admiration.

The social event of the season was the celebration of Bishop Johnson's fiftieth birthday. It was planned and executed by his family. A large banner bearing the motto, "Truth and Liberty," was suspended in mid-street, attached to ropes from the chimneys of Miller's and Johnson's houses. All the pioneers of Springville—that is, those who came the first year—were invited and a fine feast was prepared. The day was spent in reminiscences of their early travels, songs and music, and the late afternoon in dancing. A melodeon was brought to Springville by a family named Hawley, and sold to Bishop Johnson. It was a superior instrument and was used upon this occasion. Being the first instrument of the kind in town, it was the wonder of the neighborhood for months. Young people would gather at the Bishop's on Sunday evenings, to hear the music.

What was known as the Tintic War, soon broke out. Chief Tintic with his band lived and roamed mostly in the region now called Tintic. They had been troublesome since the Walker war, but an open rupture had not occurred. This season in February they stole some cattle and killed a man named John Carson. Cavalry companies were hastily organized for the pursuit and punishment of the thieves. A large party went from Springville, among whom were: George McKenzie, Proctor Humphrey, Edwin Lee, Wm. D.

Johnson, Milan Packard, Joseph Kelly and Nelson Spafford. They followed the Indians as far as the sink of the Sevier and suffered severely from the cold. This expedition was out but a short time and was successful in recovering much of the stolen stock, and the war soon ended.

In the autumn of 1856 a number of our young men were called out on the plains to establish stations for the "Y. X. Co". Governor Young had undertaken to carry the mail from Fort Leavenworth to Salt Lake City for the government. Consequently a large number of young men were called to assist in building stations and supplying them with all the necessities for a successful mail route. Among those called from Springville for those arduous labors were: Wm. D. Johnson, Samuel Pine, George McKenzie, Elmer Taylor and many others whose names cannot now be ascertained, but show-

A SCENE NORTH-WEST OF SPRINGVILLE. (Photo by Leo Hafen)

ing that our town did its full share in all the labors and perilous undertakings of those early years.

The big school house was used the winter of 1856-57 for public meetings, theaters and balls. A dramatic company was formed under the direction of Philip Westwood, the prominent members of the company being: Richard Westwood, Philip Hurst, William D. Huntington, H. M. Dougall, Semira Wood, Olive Packard, Mary Jane Matson and Bell McKenzie. "Othello," "The Lady of Lyons." "The Gypsy Farmer," and other plays were very successfully put upon the boards. The large assembly room made an excellent ballroom, for that day, wherein parties were held every two weeks.

On Christmas Eve an amusing incident occurred, which, when related, will remind some of the men now living that they were once boys, and sometimes indulged in boyish pranks. About 10 p. m., when the dance was at its height, the front doors were thrown open, and in marched fifteen youths.

A. F. MACDONALD

with policemen on each side, and were lined up for inspection in the middle of the room. They had been out "celebrating the event" in the usual manner of boys in a frontier settlement, by running loads of wood into the milldam; turning stock out; carrying off gates and otherwise making the night hideous, the police had caught them their mischief, and interrupted ious time. Wilbur Earl, chief of explained their presence, jocularly ing it was too cold for boys to be out; that hauling loads of wood was too arduous labor, and that perhaps their "mamas didn't know they were out;" therefore he and his aids had brought them to their mothers, out of the cold. A. F. McDonald, who was a man of few jokes, gave the shame-faced boys a serious lecture, which made them feel very uncomfortable. After "Mack" had finished with them, they felt as though they could have crawled through a very small knot hole. Bishop Johnson was then called to pronounce judgment then and there. They were to go at once, under the supervision of the police, and put everything in p'ace just as they had found it and if anything had been destroyed they were to restore it four fold. The penalty was fulfilled by the boys before they slept, and some said they enjoyed the reparation as well as the scattering, though one was heard to say, getting a load of wood out of the cold water of the mill pond was not a method of recreation to be chosen more than once a year.

This season members of the first hand-cart company reached Springville. Some of the belated ones came in after terrible hardships. James Holly came in three days before Christmas, just ahead of the fated hand-cart company. It was this year that Levi N. Kendall, one of Utah's pioneers, came to Springville with his family. Before New Years many of our young men, at the call of the Bishop, turned out with their teams to rescue the unfortunates. by carrying food to them and bringing them in. Among those who were brought in and taken to the home of Aaron Johnson. where they found food and shelter. were: Mrs. Kirkman and family. the James. and William Harrison families and others. They were in a pitiful condition. many having their extremities frozen. The fathers of the James and Kirkman families were left where they fell. perishing while endeavoring to push the carts in which their children rode. through the pitiless snow. Sanford Fuller. John Witbeck. Nelson Spafford and others. did gallant service in helping rescue the unfortunates from sinking into frozen graves. Joseph Loynd came in with one of the late hand-cart companies. arriving in Salt Lake late in November. He came to reside in Springville in 1858. All during the winter of 1856-7 the large rooms in the Johnson home were filled with the weary toilers. who had pushed and pulled the hand-carts with their scanty

HANNAH WOOD

fare. from the Missouri river to Salt Lake City. a distance of 1100 miles. across the snowy plains and icy mountains: through the cold sleet of the South Pass: their food growing short: their shoes giving out: their strong men falling down in the storm and dying for want of a crust of bread. and more sad than all. tender infants. starving at their mother's breasts. When news came in relation to the toilers. starving and freezing in the pitiless grasp of the storm. every available team in our village was called into requisition: freighted with warm blankets: plentiful supplies. and rushed by forced drives to rescue the unfortunates from their peril. Many never reached the Zion of their dreams. but fell beside their carts for the want of a morsel of sustaining food. When the veteran fell down between the shafts of his cart at the close of a weary day. he was laid beside his vehicle. until those who had a little life yet remaining. built a fire to thaw the icy ground and hollow out a grave. where the hapless victim was laid to rest. The next morning the survivors would resume their almost hopeless journey. leaving perhaps a father. brother or tender infant. in an icy grave beside that terrible trail. with the wild wolf and wintry blast to howl a dirge over them. It is well remembered by some living today, how wretched was the appearance of the remnant of that company. as they rested their gaunt frames upon the floors of the Johnson home. While the storm howled dismally without. the great cedar fires upon the hearths made all pleasant within. Kind hands gently administered to every want and every heart in the village beat in sympathy with the weary exiles and every hand bestowed some delicacy to nourish the emaciated forms back to life and health. We may sing and we may shout the praises of the pioneers. the Indian warriors and early settlers. each recurring 24th of July. but their trials dwindle into insignificance compared to those of the hand-cart company.

This autumn previous to the appearance of the hand-cart company. Thomas Child came to Springville. and has been a diligent and faithful worker ever since. Others who came were: Frederick Weight. our choir leader for many years: James D. Reynolds. one of our first village tailors. and Mrs. Catherine Boyer and family. The three sons. John. Philip and Francis. have been identified with our city in many capacities since.

CHAPTER XI.

THE year 1857 opened auspiciously. Our town began to take on airs of permanency. It had been thought. by some. that we would not remain long in Utah. but would move on to some other point. or journey back to Jackson county. Missouri. On the 14th of March. 1857. occurred the first tragedy to blot our fair history. We would fain pass over this dark spot. and let the foul crime be blotted from the minds of men. but like Banquo's ghost—"it will not down." There fell at this time three men: two in the middle of life. and one just having entered his man's estate. One of the victims was "Duff" Potter. a Mormon counted in good standing. and the other two. who were apostates. were Wm. Parish and his son. Beatson. The elder had been a Mormon. and in the early history of the church. his name had figured prominently. The son had also belonged to the church. but for some cause. had. like his father. withdrawn from the faith. They intended going to California and had started on their journey. it is said. that fateful night.

In that early day and. indeed. until quite recently. the word apostate. stood for all that was vile. To call a man an apostate was the epitome of all that was evil. The elder people seemed to have forgoten that they themselves were apostates from the faith of their fathers. and that a man may change his religious views. and yet not be a knave. But little has ever been ascertained as to who were the perpetrators of the bloody deed. but what has been learned the following narrative will show. It is still remembered that "Duff" Potter and William Parish had been bitter enemies to each other. since coming from their home in the east. Parish was a bold outspoken man and did not attempt to conceal his hatred for his old-time enemy. which naturally made him the object of sus-

LYMAN S. WOOD

SEMIRA WOOD

picion and dislike to some of the more zealous of the faith. It appears that Potter and one Abram Durfee pretended to apostatize, in order to get into the confidence of the Parishes. The conspirators met the Parishes, whom they completely deceived, and made them believe that they were also desirous of leaving Utah and escaping into California. Thus the scheme worked along until spring opened, when a day was fixed for their escape from Mormondom. The Parishes had some fine horses, which they had concealed beyond the "cane patch," south of town, and they were to slip away in the evening; secure the horses and by morning be far upon their journey. It was arranged by the conspirators, who evidently had outside confederates, that their families should be left behind, until such time as they could be sent for in safety. One evening, the word came to the "Little School House," where a meeting was in session, that two men had been killed, a mile and a half south of town, just east of the main road. A posse was hastily sent to the scene of slaughter, where they found the three men dead. Potter and Parish, who lay near each other, showed signs of a bloody, hand-to-hand encounter. Their guns and pistols lay close by, while their blood-stained knives told the awful tale. Both were cut horribly. Beatson Parish had run seventy-five yards from the spot where he received a shot in the heart, and was found dead in his own blood. Young Orin Parish, who was of the party, ran for his life and made his escape, but so great was his excitement that he seemed to know but little; except that as they were walking rapidly along, in single file, they were suddenly fired upon by several men in ambush, who then made a rush, and as he was not hurt he ran, following his brother, who soon fell. He jumped over a fence into a cornfield and made his way in safety to his mother's home, and could never afterward identify any one as having had any hand in the awful deed. The bodies were brought to the school house and the next day were buried. All those, who were supposed to have had a hand in the shocking affair, have gone to their final account and there we will leave them. The Parish horses were attached for debt, but were released, and later in the year Mrs. Parish and her family left Springville forever.

On the 4th of April the semi-annual municipal election was held and the returns showed the election of the following officers: Mayor—A. F. McDonald; Aldermen—Noah Packard, Myron N. Crandall, Wilbur J. Earl and Abram Day. Councilors—Lorenzo Johnson, Gideon D. Wood, William Huggins, Uriah E. Curtis, Simmons P. Curtis, H. H. Kearns, Noah T. Guyman, Spicer W. Crandall and John M. Stewart. Recorder—John M. Stewart. Chas. Drury was appointed July 12th 1858, vice John M. Stewart, resigned. Marshal—Cyrus Sanford. 1856-7

During the year 1568-7 some of the male members of the community began to follow the "fashion of the

Gentiles." by having their hair cut. This had been a distinguishing feature between Mormon or Gentile. The Indians understood this mark, and some of our plainsmen came near losing their lives by appearing with their hair cut short. When the boys began to have their locks cropped, it was preached against from the pulpit. Wm. D. Huntington told the writer, that while on a trip to California in the early years, after he had clipped his hair, he, with several others were surrounded by a band of Indians, who seemed bent upon the destruction of his party. In vain they protested that they were Mormons. The Indians pointed to their cropped heads and would not believe them. Their destruction seemed certain, when Huntington was suprised to have one of the Indians ride up to him and tore open the front of his shirt. When the Indians saw that he wore the Mormon garment, their lives and property were saved and they were allowed to proceed on their journey. It is needless to say that the locks were permitted to grow after this.

In the spring of 1857 the "big calf pasture" was purchased by the city for a city calf pasture. It comprised the tract of land at the northeast corner of the city, which is now known as the Packard farm. It served as a calf pasture for many years, but was afterwards sold to Cyrus W. Wheelock, who in turn disposed of it to Andrew Wild; then came into the hands of its present possessor.

This spring there was some signs of Indian trouble, and the people were compelled to maintain the keenest vigilance. There were special days set apart for canyon trips, when twenty or thirty teams would gather at the east gate; every man armed, and proceed in a body into the timber. While the wagons were being loaded, guards were kept on the alert, lest they be ambushed by the painted warrior. At night a guard was kept about the camp.

to prevent being surprised by the enemy, who skulked beside all the mountain trails. Guards were kept at the canyon day and night, to watch the enemy and give warning to the slumbering village. Lookouts of old men and youths not fit for guard duty, were stationed in the school house steeple, where they had an unobstructed view of the hills and could easily discern the danger signals. It was the ancient signal service they had used before. In case danger came in the night, a quick flash of fire was made and easily seen by the lookouts in the tower. If the danger was imminent, two flashes, and if the danger was actual, three flashes in quick succession. In case the danger signal was given them by the watchers in the tower, the bell was rung, calling all to arms. That old bell! How well we remember it! Its mellow tones called the village folk to hear the Sabbath talk in times of peace, and in time of war, its clang upon the midnight air, woke the people, with a

HUGH M. DOUGALL.

STATE STREET, SPRINGVILLE, IN AUGUST, 1900.

ry, from their slumbers and told them
aat the savage Indian was abroad in
he land, ready to burn and slay.
Vhen the bell gave the signal the peo-
le came hurrying to the school house,
rmed and equipped. Previous to the
se of the big bell, the people were
rought together by the bellman, who,
iounted on a fleet horse, would ride
irough the village ringing his bell.
: would surprise the people of this
ay to see how quickly the people
oull be brought together. One in-
tance will illustrate. One evening in
357, Orson Hyde drove to Springville
om Salt Lake and said that he would
old a meeting if the Saints could be
onvened. H. M. Dougall, who stood
ear, was immediately commissioned to
pread the news. He mounted "old
ack" and taking Johnson's large din-
er bell, rode through the streets ring-
ng his bell and shouting—"Elder
lyde will preach tonight, at early can-

dle-light." After supper| the elder
found a large congregation awaiting
him. There was just enough excitement during the season to keep the people on the alert, and by this alertness
probably saved life and property. The
cow herd went upon the Union bench
under a strong guard each day. This
herd commenced to gather at the north
gate at six o'clock, and drove slowly
southward. The herdman's horn commenced its blast, as a signal that the
herd had started, and the cows would
commence to gather on Main street,
driven by the barefooted boys and girls
of the town, accompanied by their
many dogs. In the evening the notes
of the horn would again be heard
throughout the town, telling that the
cows had come home.

This year an invitation was sent, by
Governor Young, to the various towns
in Utah county to join Salt Lake county in celebrating the tenth anniversary

of the pioneers coming into Utah. The celebration was to be held at the head of Big Cottonwood canyon. Some twenty teams, headed by the band in their fine new band wagon, went from Springville. This was the third brass band organized in Springville and a most excellent organization it was. Richard Prator, a good musician from London, was the leader. Wm. D. Huntington was drum major, and made quite an inposing appearance in his uniform, high cap and baton. The members, so far as can be recalled, were: Henry Moss, Joseph Lyons, George Williams, Henry Roylance, Wm. C. Huntington, Wm. Cordingly, Charley Stevenson, Fred Weight, Thos. Burnett, Thos. Snelson and Wm. Clyde, who beat the bass drum. Loren Roundy, who was the owner of some fine horses, was teamster. Many of the old-timers will remember this fine turn-out parading the streets and making sweet music, each recurring holiday, while the barefooted boys ran along behind, longing for the day when they would be men and perhaps beat the big drum and ride in the band wagon.

On the morning of July 22nd, the train gathered in front of Johnson's home, and just as old Sol shot his golden arrows into the valley it started with the band playing and the flag flying. The present road across Provo bench was marked off that day for future travel, but it had previously passed up the present dugway, then extended two miles north, coming upon the bench east of Pleasant Grove. Bishop Johnson had walked home from Salt Lake the fall previous and had come along where the road should have been, according to his judgment. He drove his team in the lead, turning to the left of the old road, upon the first bench, going northwest to a little hollow leading upon the main flat, then showing Andrew Wild, who rode on horseback, a large stake at the Pleasant Grove end of the road, that had

been previously set, told him to keep his eye upon the mark and ride straight. The teams followed making a plain track. That night they camped at the mouth of Big Cottonwood canyon. The evening was spent in contests by various bands; among the number being the famous Nauvoo brass band. Next day the long train wended its way up to the beautiful valley at the head of the canyon, where tents were pitched under the spreading branches of the towering pines. The next day will never be forgotten by those present. There was a battery of artillery that kept the echos ringing from daybreak until 8 p. m. A fine programme was carried out, while dancing, swinging and feasting, was kept up until the "wee" hours of the 25th. It was upon this occasion that A. O. Smoot and Porter Rockwell rode into camp, sunburned and travel stained, and imparted the startling news that Johnson's army was on the way to Utah.

The people returned home on the 26th. Now was a time of real excitement. A large army was on the way; for what purpose could only be conjectured. The journey would be long and the march must naturally be slow, so the people had time to collect their wits, and decide upon a line of procedure. Brigham Young, then the governor, ordered a thorough organization of the militia, which was accordingly done and Aaron Johnson was appointed brigadier general of the Peteetneet Military district, and he arranged the district into regiments, battalions, etc. Martial law was proclaimed by Governor Young. Companies were organized in Springville and arms, ammunition, pack saddles, etc., were prepared for the notable expedition to Echo canyon, where Governor Young was determined to make an effort to withstand the "army of invasion," until their purpose of coming was fully demonstrated.

Two companies marched from our town to help stem the tide of the invading army. The wildest stories were afloat of the intentions of the coming army. One of the most disquieting was to the effect that they intended to hang Governor Young and the Mormon leaders. A song was composed by local talent, that became very popular, and showed the spirit of the people. The chorus was:

> "Then let us be on hand,
> By Brigham Young to stand
> And if our enemies do appear.
> We'll sweep them from the land."

It was a sad sight to see the boys march to Echo canyon to swell the host which was determined to keep the army at bay until assured of its peaceful intention. And in case it should prove that its intent was hostile, to withstand it to the death, if necessary. No shouting thousands assembled with music, banners and hurrahs, to inspire them to do their duty, but they marched silently away shoulder to shuolder. with a grim look upon their faces—to do and die, if, necessary, for what they believed to be right.

It is not our intention to state any of the causes which led to Johnson's army being sent to Utah; that has been already written in the various history of Utah, but to refer to it as an incident in Springville's history. The Echo canyon expedition cost Springville $8,000.

Early this year the big pasture was fenced off by itself and given by the various owners to the public. Previously it had been farmed, but in consequence of the alkali in the soil, it was abandoned. It was thought to be a safer place to turn the cattle, than the Union bench, as it was so far from the canyon where the Indians roved. The principal donors of the pasture lands, were: William Miller, Aaron Johnson, Myron Crandall, Richard Bird, John W. Deal and Wm. Mendenhall. It was agreed that all the men between the age of eighteen and forty-five should do a certain amount of fencing, when all should own it as a pasture, and all who

came afterward were permitted to use it without price. A fortification was built, up in Spring creek canyon, to prevent the Indians from driving the stock into the mountains by that route. It was called Miller's Fort, because Wm. Miller had charge of the work.

This autumn the "Reformation" was inaugurated and raged the winter of 1857-8. The Saints were called upon to "repent and humble themselves before God, and He would deliver them from their enemies." Some of the more impetuous became quite frantic in their religious fervor. "All who are not for us, are against us," and, "It may be necessary to cleanse the platter," were quotations frequently uttered by some whose zeal had run into fanaticism. A sort of father confessorship was inaugurated, where the penitents might go and divulge to the father confessor their short comings and be forgiven. All over eight years of age were required to visit this confessional and there lay before the High Priest their iniquities. One confessional was appointed for each ward; that for the fourth ward being in the south chamber of Bishop Johnson's house. A place of baptism was established in the millrace, just in front of where Packard Bro's store now stands, and here nearly all over eight years "renewed their covenants."

The home guard took turns sleeping in the Little school houre and at 8 o'clock every morning, all the militia of the town turned out for drill, roll call and to hear the bulletins from the seat of war which were brought in daily by pony express. Col. Lot Smith and Gen. Burton were out on the Big Sandy, with a few mounted scouts, harrassing the enemy and occasionally cutting out and driving off oxen and mules used in the transportation of ammunition and supplies, which stock was passed into the valley for safe keeping. Every day news of what the boys were doing in Echo canyon were read to the men, formed in a hollow square, for roll call. and cheers were given with a hearty good will when news came of some brilliant coup having been made out upon the Sandy by the boys at the front. Robert Watson was the adjutant of the company. and when a person was absent. a pin pricked a hole in the paper opposite his name. It is only necessary to add that not a very formidable array of names were "pricked."

CHAPTER XII.

DURING the early autumn of 1857. our town presented quite a martial aspect. There were drills upon the square every Saturday until the volunteers became quite proficient in the arts of war. A discharged soldier, by the name of Nethercoat. went through the county giving semiweekly drills in fencing. He was an expert with the sword and over fifty of the men and boys took a course under him: all armed with wooden swords. When wooden swords were not used. sticks served the purpose. and the boys were ingaged in "right and left cut. point and parry." for months. On Saturday evenings the drills usually terminated by the boys choosing sides and having a match engagement. Swords for actual service were made of sawmill saws. forged at Sidney Roberts' smithy.

Late in the autumn the people were thrown into a state of excitement and sorrow by the loss of the little daughter of Mr. and Mrs. Sidney Roberts. Mr. Roberts will be remembered as quite a genius in a mechanical way. He had a machine shop standing upon the spot now occupied by the North Co-op.. He made the first separator and threshing machine ever used in Springville: and he also made a machine for cutting nails. This little Roberts girl. who was about four years old, was last seen near Hobble creek. about dark. and as she did not return. her parents became alarmed and the neighbors were notified and all joined in the search. The creek was dragged quite to the lake. by the anxious searchers. and every part of the city was examined. but the child was never found. It was thought by many that some of the numerous emigrants that passed through our town that autumn. had stolen her. and by others that she had strayed off into the west field and had been devoured by the large wolves that invested that region.

In the fall of 1857 the first peaches ever grown in Springville. ripened on the trees that stood on the corner of

WILLIAM D. HUNTINGTON

Bishop Johnson's lot. In 1851 some peach pits had been planted by the Bishop and quite a large orchard was set out. though many had no faith in its ultimate bearing. This spring the trees blossomed beautifully and bore a fine lot of peaches, and many of the townspeople got a taste of the luscious fruit. By 1861 there were more peaches in the town than could be used. The first fruit in the town to be really cultivated. was the wild currants. obtained from Spanish Fork canyon. After a few years cultivation they became very large and were used both dried and fresh. as the main household fruit. The ground cherries were also gathered and dried. and when brought forth in the winter. made excellent sauce and pies. Dried squash pies and pumpkin butter helped out the winter fare. and beet molasses furnished most of the sweetening. Sugar was a real luxury. at this time. being 45 cents per pound. It was sel-

BISHOP WILLIAM BRINGHURST

dom that the boys and girls ever tasted a cake made with sugar. 'n those days. but in a few years sugarcane was introduced and sorgum was plentiful. The old-fashioned candy pulling then became the rage. and the young people would meet at Sanford's. Deal's. Bird's or Crandall's. play "snap and catch 'em" and enjoy themselves as only youths. who are free from care. can. when there is plenty of candy and a fellow has his best girl by his side. The boys with literary inclinations would meet in some room and by the light of a birch bark torch would sit around the hearth. and one would read aloud some borrowed book while the others roasted potatoes in the hot ashes. or popped corn. until a late hour. The boys and girls would also have an occasional dance in some large room. procured for the auspicious occasion. A large room at Edward Hall's home: a front room at Widow Humphrey's. and the little adobe school house. in the "fort row." were among the popular resorts. Half a dozen boys would furnish a candle each. others a peck of

CYRUS SANFORD

SPRINGVILLE IN AUGUST. 1900, LOOKING SOUTHEAST FROM REYNOLDS' STORE

wheat each and others. produce. such as any one of the three village fiddlers. Benjamin Blanchard. William Smith or Levi Curtis. could be induced to take in payment for their services. and all was ready for the dance. Early candle-light was the usual hour for commenc-ing and midnight for closing. It did not take the boys and girls as long to prepare for a ball then. as now. They had not so many nice clothes to put on. The boys often had to borrow their mother's shoes. which. when well black-ened with soot from the under side of a stove lid. made a dancing shoe not to be dispised. Then with their linsey shirts tucked into their home-made jeans pants. and with well buttered locks. they were ready for the ball room. The first couple to arrive lighted their candle and put it in the wooden bracket. and so on until all had arrived. The fiddlers came and then the dance began in real earnest and continued till mid-night. when good-byes were said and all made for home.

During the autumn of 1857. John M. Stewart. who was one of the Bishop's counselors. became much dissatisfied with the state of affairs. as well as many others. among whom may be mentioned: Zepheniah Warren. Ezra Parish. Murdock McKinzie. Smith Humphery and Henry Brooks. Stew-art was more outspoken than the oth-ers and. therefore. incurred the enmity of the more fanatical. Some of the po-licemen. then twelve in number. were said to be rather mischievious and one or two were downright mean. They played some tricks on certain of the back-sliders that seemed very funny to them. but very grave to the victims. The teachers. some of whom belonged to the police force. in going among the people found out how they felt in re-gard to religious matters. While be-ing catechised in regard to prayer. Warren acknowledged that he did not pray. for as he explained he "did not believe in bothering God about such a little matter as blessing a meal of vict-nals." A few nights after Werren was called out by one of the police. an ex-officio teacher. and was quite surprised to find himself in the midst of a squad of the semi-civil and ecclesiastical authorities. With mysterious signs, he was taken out over the fort wall, east of the city, to a melon patch. A large melon was plucked, cut open, and all seated themselves around it, when the leader said: "Brother Warren, will you please ask the blessing? "Brother" Warren would, and did, making the best prayer of his life. The melon was then eaten and the victim of the joke escorted, in the same silent manner, back to his home. Warren left for California in the spring after the advent of Johnson's army, and he declared until the day of his death, that he thought he was taken out to be killed that night. John M. Stewart declared that his life had been threatened and fearful lest the threat should be carried out, he left one night, not even saying goodbye to his family. It was late in the season and he intended joining the soldiers out at Ham's Fork, in their winter encampment. He went up the left fork of Hobble creek, intending to go over and cross the head of Provo canyon, but in the dark and storm he mistook his way, and came along the ridge between Provo and Hobble creek canyons to Dry canyon, and came out at the mouth of Hobble creek, just where he had started. All that day he skulked along the mountains working toward Provo canyon, which he attempted to pass that night, but was captured by the guard stationed there to prevent persons, without orders, passing that way. Bishop Johnson was informed of his capture, by a special courier, and the Bishop hastily called the band together, and with a few friends, met the runaway, between our city and Provo, and escorted him to the Bishop's residence where a long talk was held and Stewart's safety being pledged, he returned to his home. The next spring he went to Camp Floyd and worked for the soldiers long enough to get an outfit, when he left for California. Within the next two years the old set-

tlers who left for California, were: Orin Craw and the Whitlock family.

During this autumn a dog killing mania seemed to prevail. It was charged that the canine appetite for mutton was very strong, and that many sheep had been stolen by the dogs of the town. Like every other reform, wisdom did not always dictate and the good dogs were killed along with the worthless curs. Very bad feelings were engendered and several serious encounters were narrowly averted. Teacher's trials were called to settle the difficulty, and as it was hard to separate the policeman from his religious duties, the police were usually sustained and the slaughter went on until there were but few dogs left in town. The pet dogs were kept housed, but still the dog killers tried to get at them. Carlo, Richard Turpin's pet dog, was sent where his fondness for mutton would bother him no more, upon which event, Philip Westwood wrote a poem which he read in a public meeting, causing a good deal of laughter and applause. He moved, shortly afterward, to California.

The year 1858 was made notable by the "move." During the first months of the new year, negotiations had been going on with the army, to find out what was their object in coming and what they intended to do, but nothing satisfactory had been ascertained. Governor Young called upon the people to be ready to leave their homes in the north and move south, setting fire to their homes if necessary, and to lay the country waste before the advancing army, in case satisfactory terms could not be made. Scouting parties had been sent south during the winter, to seek a place of refuge for the people, if the occasion demanded. All the wheat in our settlement, except seed grain, was ground and put into barrels, ready for transportation if necessary. All the coopers in town were rushed with work, preparing barrels that would

ALEXANDER ROBERTSON

hold 200 pounds of flour each. These barrels were made of straight-grained pine, three feet long, and split into staves, then shaved down to proper thickness with the draw knife; jointed upon the edges and hooped with small oak, split in the middle. Simeon Blanchard and Cyrus Wingate, who were the pioneer coopers, and Rufus Fisher, whose cooperage was stationed at the bridge, did this work. These men had for years previously, made all the woodenware for the town, tubs, churns, etc. The old mill had been running night and day, reducing the wheat to flour, which was transferrd and pounded into the barrels, ready for the exodus. Much of the flour was tramped into barrels by barefooted boys, whose feet had been scrubbed and sandpapered for the occasion. These barrels, with their precious contents were stored at various centers all ready for quick loading in case a move was ordered. All the tithing wheat was ground and stored under the stage in the east end of the Big school house. Wagons were

repaired; tents mended, and every preparation made for a general exodus. It was determined to make Utah as much of a desert as it was when the pioneers first saw it, rather than to allow it to be a place of succor for their enemies.

Three hundred families came to Springville, from the north, during the season; some made their homes here, among them were: Solomon D. Chase and family; Dorr P. Curtis, E. P. Brinton, Henry Mower, Sr. and family; Richard Thorn, John Waters and E. H. Kindred. The latter was the first wagon maker, to follow his trade permanently, in Springville. The Springville people opened their homes to the refugees and many built homes in various places for temporary use. The bastions, at the four gates of the city, were roofed in, affording comfortable shelters for the wanderers. All along the banks of the creek, on the public square and on all the vacant lots, circular houses, built of cane and thatched with rushes, were erected. The outside streets, next to the town, and some of the narrow streets on the outside blocks, were set aside as garden plots for the strangers. The population of our city was doubled this spring, but most of the new comers returned to their homes in the autumn.

In the fall of 1858, more money was in circulation than ever before. The army had, by stipulation, constructed their barracks in Cedar valley, west of the lake and named the place Camp Floyd. A vast amount of supplies of every kind was needed to feed them and to build comfortable quarters for this army of four thousand. Nearly ever man in Springville went over to the camp to work, or to sell farm produce to the soldiers. While money was plentiful, its buying capacity was small, for instance. Youths' boots were from $12 to $16 per pair; calicos and domestics, 75 cents per yard; nails, 60 cents per pound; 8x10 window glass, cents per pane: tobacco, tea and coffee, were way out of sight. At this time and for some years before and after, our mothers and sisters had spun, woven and made, nearly all the wearing apparel for the families. Nearly every family owned sheep that were herded in bands in various localities during eight months of the year and then folded during the winter at their various homes. The wool was scoured; carded into rolls and then twisted into yarn by the old spinning wheel, propelled by the women of the families. The hum of the spinning wheel could be heard from the rising of the sun, to the going down thereof. Later a carding machine was set up at Provo and carded the wool into rolls, ready for the deft hands of the spinner. The old hand loom made the web and woof into jeans and linseys. This work occupied all the months of the spring and summer until September, when the garments were cut out and made, ready

for winter use. Fine, comfortable shirts they made, too, in those days, when the girls wore woolen dresses and the boys wore trousers of tow. With interminable pains did the mothers prepare the clothes for their families! Oftimes the boy's clothes were darned and patched, until the original fabric could hardly be ascertained. The household cloths, such as table linen, sheets, towels, etc., were made of flax; the preparing of which was a tiresome and difficult task. First, the soil in which it was planted, had to be prepared with great care; then weeded over and over again and when ripe, pulled and tied into small bundles. It was threshed by striking the heads over a pole and then placed in water which rotted the outside straw, then taken out and dried in the sun. It was afterward broken upon an implement constructed for the purpose; heckled to remove the tow from the fibre, when it was ready for the spinning upon the

CITY HALL. BUILT IN 1880. USED ALSO AS A THEATER.

BISHOP NEPHI PACKARD

foot wheel and distaff. The stuff for the boy's shirts and blouses, was woven with linen warp and tow filling; colored with a preparation of copperas and rabbit weed which made, at first, a respectable color, but alas! in a short time every vistage of the original color was gone, leaving it about the color of the dust in the road.

Herding the cows was a very important occupation during the summer months and fell mostly to the boys. The presence of the soldiers had a re-straining influence upon the "Lamanites" and it was not considered dangerous for the boys to go to the herding grounds with the cows, even as far as the second bridge in the canyon. The most luxuriant grass grew in that locality in those days. It was difficult for the cows to walk home at night, their udders were so distended with milk. The boys were generally paid 2 cents a head per day for herding. If the cows were left out a night the boys were

docked 4 cents per cow, which made them more diligent. The herd boy began to study human nature at that early day by watching the cows. Those who were treated kindly at home, at the milking time, were anxious to get home and be "pailed," while those that were kicked and "jawed" had to be driven home and safely closed in, else they would go off and hide and the herd boy would be minus his 4 cents, for that day. The picture of the herd boy still hangs familiarly on memory's wall. The tow pants and shirt, in which he could roll in the dust and not change the color, and his cap, made out of what had served his father many years as a coat or vest; the visor made of a piece of boot top. He was always barefooted and with the bottoms of his feet so calloused, that he could prance like a wild horse of the pampas, over the flinty ground without getting a bruise. His greasy dinner sack, containing his noonday lunch, hung around his neck; in his hand he carried a sling, with which to throw stones at the roving stock and thrust into his belt was the indispensible "sego digger"—and there you have the plucky herd boy of 1858. Their only method of making fires, was by carrying slow-burning "buffalo chips" to the herd ground, and there the fire was kept burning for weeks, by keeping it covered at night. Sometimes the boys took roasting ears, potatoes and eggs, to cook in the embers and sometimes a luckless bird or rabbit, which fell a victim to their slings, added their appetizing qualities to the meal. Four months of this year the chief rendezvous of the herd boys was at the first bridge, where the camp fires were never permitted to go out. Here a "Crusoe cave" was excavated and used as a shelter against rain. The cows were allowed to go far up the canyon and the boys would take turn about in going after them, while the contingent at the dugway kept them together until all were in, and then they came

THE CENTRAL SCHOOL HOUSE. BUILT IN 1892. COST $17,500.

slowly home. Several times during the summer the roving Indians relieved the boys of their dinner. Upon such occasions the boys considered themselves lucky, with only the loss of their dinner. One day, just before noon, as the boys were gathered at the cave, they were started by the sight of several Indians coming down the canyon. One of the boys seized the dinner sacks and ran down the stream, where he hid them under the dry leaves and returned without having been seen by the redmen, and sat down demurely among his chums. The Indians rode up and one called out, "Gimme biscuit." A herd boy replied. "Haint' got none." "You lie!" savagely cried the man with an appetite. "No, me got no biscuit," said the boy, whose courage began to leak out, at the savage looks of the Indian. "Ugh! me see," said the native; and he dismounted, peered into the cave; examined the ground for tracks, and then started along the path and went straight to the spot of concealment and brought the dinner sacks back amid yells of delight from his companions. He divided the biscuits with the boys and rode away.

The author is here reminded of the difficulty experienced in keeping fires burning upon the hearths, during the first ten years. Matches were rare and very costly and in those days were put up in little, round, wooden boxes, the length of the match: a box containined fifty lucifers and retailed at 50 cents. The last member of a family to go to bed at night would carefully cover the coals with ashes and the first one up in the morning would take the ashes off and kindle the fire. Sometimes not a spark of fire remained: then one of the children would be sent to a house, from whose chimney smoke could be seen issuing, to borrow some coals. The cooking was largely done upon the hearths, in a frying pan, pot and dutch oven. The old-fashioned crane was attached to the fireplace, by a swivle, upon which bubbled the tea kettle.

In this year of the "move" Nicholas Grosebeck came to reside in Springville and opened a dry goods store in some rooms on the fort row. G. D. Wood & Son had previously opened a store, and Henry H. Kearns had carried a small stock in 1856-7, in the house now owned by George McKenzie. Wm. J. Stewart was, however, the very first merchant in Springville, having kept store in the old fort as early as 1852. In 1853 a man by the name of Geo. W. Johnson kept a dry good store, where he also sold drugs, home-made and imported inks, and a few toilet articles.

CHAPTER XIII.

IN the spring of 1859 there was an unusual excitement over the city election. Heretofore things had gone along with very few hitches. Many of the more liberal ones were tired of blending the teacher's calling with that of the policeman, thereby bringing continual clashing between the civil and ecclesiastical authorities, which oftimes had caused very bitter feeling. A sort of a compromise was effected and the following officers were elected: Mayor—Lorenzo Johnson; Aldermen—Wilber J. Earl, A. F. McDonald, Richard Bird and Orin Craw. Councilors—Cyrus H. Wheelock, John C. Whitbeck, Noah T. Guyman, Wm. Robinson, Gideon D. Wood, Spicer Crandall, Abram Day, Cyrus Sanford and Simmons P. Curtis. Recorder—Charles H. Drury. Marshal—Wm. D. Johnson.

On the 11th of April in consequence of the Kolob episode, and the enforced absence of nearly every official in the town, the City Council was re-organized by appointment, with the following officers: Mayor—Abram Day. Aldermen—A. P. Murry, H. H. Cole, William Wordsworth and Orin Craw. Councilors—Moses Clawson, Wm. Huggins, Ransom Potter, David A. Curtis, Cyrus H. Wheelock, Wm. Robinson, Spicer Crandall and John C. Whitbeck. Recorder—Martin P. Crandall; Charles D. Evans was appointed October 2nd, vice

Crandall, resigned. Marshal—Samuel C. Pine; Cyrus Sanford was appointed, vice Pine, resigned, and was succeeded by Thomas Dallin, December 22nd, by appointment. Wm. Mendenhall was appointed alderman, January 21, 1860, to succeed Orin Craw, resigned. March 31, 1860, Geo. B. Matson was appointed councilor, vice David A. Curtis, resigned, and S. C. Perry in place of Ransom Potter. Wm. Wordsworth was appointed mayor, pro tem., vice Abram Day, who then moved to Fairview, Sanpete county.

On the 8th of March, 1859, Associate Justice John Craddlebaugh, came to Provo to hold a term of court. Alexander Wilson was United States prosecuting attorney and Peter Dotson marshal. The court appointed Lucius Scoville clerk. Two companies of United States soldiers, including a battery of light artillery, came as an escort and to insure fair play. A grand jury was empanelled, to inquire into the high crimes and misdemeanors that were alleged to have been committed in this district. Among the members of that grand jury, summoned from Springvile, were: Lorenzo Johnson, Noah T. Guyman and Wilbur J. Earl. Judge Craddlebaugh delivered a most astonishing charge to the grand jury, in which this passage appeared: "You are the tools: the dupes; the instruments, of a tyrannical church despotism. The heads of your church order and direct you. You are taught to obey their orders, and commit those horrid murders (before referred to). Deprived of your liberties, you have lost your manhood, and become the willing instruments of bad men. I say unto you, it will be my earnest effort, while among you to knock off your ecclesiastical shackles and set you free." As may be supposed, with such a charge to such a jury, no indictments were found. The court discharged the grand jury, and sat in chambers, where he issued his bench warrants for many prominent men in Utah county, including all the civil, military and ecclesiastical authorities of Springville, for the killing of the Parishes and Forbes. An amusing incident occurred in Springville during the session of court, that will show the state of affairs and illustrate how deceitful are appearances. An old resident, who was called an apostate and had undergone some persecution at the hands of the police, rushed over to Provo and reported to the marshal that a foul murder had been committed in Rock canyon. He explained, in his excitement, that early that morning he had seen Edward Hall, Jos. Bartholomew and Zepheniah Warren, the two former with ropes, knives and axes, and the latter with a chain around his neck, going up Rock canyon. In about two hours, he said, Hall and Bartholomew had returned without Warren, who, he alleged had been murdered. Some officers were dispatched to Springville to investigate the mystery. They visited

ROMANZO A. DEAL.

Warren's home and found him just returned with a jag of wood, and, upon further investigation, found that Hall and his partner had gone up the canyon after their horses, in company with Warren, but had returned before him.

The authorities at Springville, having "friends at court," found out that in all probability they would be arrested and taken to the military prison at Camp Floyd, so they took a walk by night and when the posse came, about March 20th, to make the arrest, they were gone. The writer well remmembers the early morning of March 20th. A cold blizzard had raged all night and just at daybreak there came a loud rap at the door. Instantly all was stir and bustle in the Johnson home. The tramping outside and the jingling of sabres, as the house was being surrounded, indicated that something unusual was going on out there and in a moment there was a face at every window upstairs, and, behold, there in front of the house were two hundred dragoons in military array and on the east and west was a cordon of Uncle Sam's boys in blue, with glittering guns and sabres, on the alert that none should escape. Mary Johnson answered the summons and was informed that they had a warrant for the arrest of Bishop Johnson. Marshal Dotson did the talking, Marshal Stone being his aid. The soldiers were told that Mr. Johnson was not at home and that his whereabouts was not known. But they held a search warrant and respectfully demanded entrance. Mary asked a few moments in which to prepare the family for inspection and the officers readily granted her request. The house contained thirty-five rooms, to say nothing of cellars and garrets. In a few minutes the family was prepared and the marshal, with his deputies, went carefully through the building. Of course their search was fruitless and after apologizing for performing their unpleasant duty, they retired. The

"assembly" was sounded by the bugler and the troops gathered from different parts of the town and proceeded up the canyon, as far as the forks, in the hail and snow. At the mouth of the canyon they met a herd boy and asked him if he had seen any tracks, up the canyon. "Yes! lots of 'em." replied the boy. So they went on quite a distance and not seeing any tracks, they returned and meeting the same boy, told him he had lied, for there was not one human track in that canyon. "Oh!" said the boy, with a twinkle in his eye, "I never said nothin' about human tracks, it was rabbit tracks I seen." At Richard Bird's they made an arrest and thought they had Dick for sure, but when they brought the man up town, it proved to be a nephew by the name of Kelsey Bird, who was living there. In the evening the tired dragoons returned to Provo disgusted, after their wild-goose chase. A. F. McDonald and H. H. Kearns, who had been arrested a few days before, were, according to popular rumor, strapped across a cannon and taken to Camp Floyd by the returning squadron, where they were confined for six months in a loathsome prison. About the 15th of October they were permitted to return home for a week's visit to their families. They were under the care of Wm. Wall, a deputy marshal, and one evening as he was returning his prisoners, they made a leap for liberty and succeeded in making their escape in the darkness. Several shots were fired after them, as they made their way towards the mountains, where they joined the Kolob boys, at their rendezvous at the head of Day's canyon.

Our authorities' first hiding place was at the head of Big Cottonwood canyon, but they were compelled to move frequently, because the army was on the constant lookout for them. For two months they were camped in Kolob, within sight of the town and with a splendid view of the whole valley. At that time Kolob was a beautiful place. There were stately, tall maples, under which grew a green sward dotted with flowers and down the little ravine sparkled a mountain stream. Under the cool shade the camp was pitched and a lookout established which commanded a view of the valley. In the night squads took turns in visiting their homes, where they would remain for a few days, keeping out of sight, and then return with supplies to their mountain retreat. Thus the summer was passed, dodging hither and thither, until late autumn, when an understanding was arrived at, between the military and civil officers, and the Kolob boys returned to their homes. The word Kolob, in Mormon lore, means "highest heaven," the place where Elohim resides and the name was given to our beautiful mountain retreat by Bishop Johnson. Geo. A. Smith said, in the Springville meeting house in the winter of 1859, that General Aaron Johnson and his men in Kolob had held the army in check, for it was the belief at Camp Floyd, that General Johnson was in the mountains with a great number of men, located in bands, from Cache valley to Sanpete, ready to check any move that might be made by the army. A bit of history may appropriately recorded here, as narrated by General Johnson.

During the summer of 1859 the soldiers at Camp Floyd, became impatient to do something to break the monotomy of camp life. From spies, who constantly beset the camp, as peddlers, it was ascertained that Albert Sydney Johnston contemplated making a night march to Salt Lake City and take up his quarters there. It was said that the move was actually planned and that arms were inspected and equipments put in order for the important expedition. In case such a march should have been started, notice would have been given and a check interposed. Generals Wells and Burton, with the

militia of Salt Lake county, were to meet the advancing columns at the point of the mountain, as a sruprise party; and General Johnson with minute men from Utah county, was to attack the fort at Floyd and capture it, by a flank movement around the lake. However, General Johnston did not attempt to march to Salt Lake City; owing to the fact that he knew the Mormons in the mountains, under General Aaron Johnson, would make it warm for him.

The spiritual wants of the people were administered to, this summer, by Cyrus H. Wheelock and how satisfactorily it was done will be remembered to this day. He was a most eloquent preacher and a great favorit with the people. The civil rights were adequately protected by Abram Day, as mayor, and Samuel Pine, as marshal. After the return of Aaron Johnson from his "summer vacation" he, with his counselors, Wm. Miller and M. N. Crandall, resumed sway in the bishopric.

In the winter of 1859-60 there was a big sleigh ride projected and carried out. The snow had fallen to a great depth, and the sleighing was at its best. Everything on runners was out; from the large bob-sleigh with its load of happy people, to the boy and pony with a hand-sled attached to a 40-foot rope, also the band in their fine turnout. The poor were not forgotten, nor those who had no teams, but all were taken out for a ride and everybody enjoyed it to the utmost.

The Big school house was opened this winter for theaters and balls, and a series of lectures and debates was held, in addition to the Sabbath Day services. Thus passed the first decade of Springville settlement. From a few families it had grown to hundreds and all looked favorable to a bright and peaceful future.

In the spring of 1860 William Miller was called to go to Provo, to act as Bishop, and the people felt that they had lost a tried and faithful man, who had done much to make Springville what it was. During this year the militia was more thoroughly organized and much drilling in field movements and manual of arms was engaged in. Dorr P. Curtis was the presiding genius of the town, in the matter of military drills, etc., and every Saturday company, battalion and squad drill, were executed upon the public square. There was a cavalry company under the command of Captain Wm. Bringhurst, with fifty men, well equipped: besides two companies of infantry. Arms and uniforms were purchased, at great private expense, and much enthusiasm manifested. The Branch was called upon to furnish four teams and two yoke of oxen, to proceed to Little Cottonwood canyon, to haul rock for the temple, then in course of construction. These teams were furnished on donation by the ward and the teamsters were also paid by general subscription. For several years these teams were employed. Thomas Child, the head teacher, usually had charge of raising and fitting out these teams, and he performed many days of arduous labor along this line. A mass meeting would be called and the call read to the people. After some deliberation, one would furnish a wagon: another an ox: another a yoke, and so on, until everything needed was forthcoming. Then came the real work, which fell to Mr. Child and his assistant teachers, of gathering these things together and sending them off. The mothers and daughters of the village, did their proportion by donating their homespun socks and mittens for the teamsters.

During the turbulent times of 1859 some bad feelings had arisen between the brethren in regard to church matters, but after the old regime was again inaugurated, an era of good feeling had been ushered in, and the Fourth of July was celebrated with unusual ceremony. At a mass meeting one

Sunday afternoon, about the middle of June, volunteers were called for to open the road into the righthand fork of Hobble creek canyon and to get a liberty pole for the Fourth. Thirty young men with wagons and oxen, headed by Wm. D. Huntington and with Daniel Stanton as chief teamster, went into the canyon and stayed there two nights, returning with a fine pole, which, when planted, stood out of the ground 105 feet. One Saturday afternoon, before the Fourth, the entire population turned out for the raising. All the ropes in the city were gathered up, together with chains: a load of long poles for props: a block-and-tackle to raise the liberty pole. A large wooden fish was attached to the top of the pole for a weather vane. When all was ready Wm. D. Huntington gave the word of command and the pole was raised into place and the ground around it tramped down hard, and then three rousing cheers were given. The rest of the day was spent in games. Some days afterward, a very large eagle flew

JAMES E. HALL

into town from the south and lighted upon the pole, where he sat until some unsympathetic hunter took a shot at him, and he flew away, with a loud scream. This splendid pole served for two years, when one night some mischievious party bored it full of holes, a few feet above the ground and it fell soon after. It was then cut in the center and used as a foot-bridge across the creek during the flood of 1862.

Our city was horrified, early in the spring of 1860, by the killing of Jack Cole and Levi Davis. Cole was charged with having purloined some government mules from Camp Floyd. A warrent had been sworn out and delivered to Jesse Steele, captain of police, for his arrest. Cole had grown up in Springville and was well known and thought to be a desperate character. He always went about well armed and was a dead shot. Captain Steele took a posse of eight men, including Levi Davis, to make the arrest. They went to his father's home, just before sunrise, and upon inquiring, found that the culprit was in bed. The captain went into the room where Cole was making his toilet and read the warrant to him. Jack said, "All right, I'll be out in a minute." Steele returned to the door-yard where his posse awaited him and in a moment Cole came to the door with a revolver in each hand, when Steele slipped up to him, and said, "Jack, I must have those pistols." Just at that moment Levi Davis made a movement as if to draw a pistol and Cole, quick as a flash, fired at Davis and mortally wounded him. Then the posse opened fire upon the desperado and he fell with eight bullets in his body. None others of the posse were hit. Davis died eight days after. Cole expired on the same day.

The year 1861 passed away quietly. The people made many improvements. A vast amount of canyon work was done: Sunday schools and day schools were maintained and many social gatherings were held. This spring, Edward Starr, Sylvanus Hewlet and others, were called to go to Dixie, for the purpose of building up that region and especially to raise cotton, it having been ascertained that cotton of a very superior quality could be grown in the southern part of the territory. At the spring election there was a break in the usual unanimity that had marked the previous ones. A mass meeting had been called for the purpose of nominating the city officials and a ticket was chosen. There had been a feeling growing for some time.

HUNGERFORD ACADEMY (PRESBYTERIAN). BUILT IN 1886. COST $9,000.

against "chronic office holding" and the people determined to put a stop to it. At this time the city was deeply in debt, through the building of various school houses and other public buildings and a series of warants had been issued, which had depreciated in value, selling as low as 25 cents on the dollar. At the caucus, this spring, these matters were discussed with considerable warmth; one party declaring that if elected, they would not only serve the city gratuitously, but would give to the city treasury all the warrants in their possession and would work indefatigably to relieve the city of the load of debt. The contest was a warm one and resulted in the election of the following ticket: Mayor—Wm. D. Huntington. Aldermen—Lyman S. Wood, W. J. Stewart, Abram Noe and Joseph W. Bissell. Councilors—Solomon D. Chase, O. B. Huntington, Milan Packard, Henry Mower, John B. Atchinson, James Oakley, George McKinzie, Sylvanus Hewlet and Richard Thorn. Recorder—Wm. M. Bromley. Marshal—Joseph Kelley. It is but just to say that those officers carried out their pledges to the very letter and the city's indebtedness was much reduced.

This spring excitement was caused when the news was flashed over the Union telegraph line that Fort Sumter had been bombarded by the rebels and the War of the Rebellion was on in earnest. At this time a tri-weekly mail was run south from Salt Lake City and the coming of each mail was anxiously looked forward to by many. At this time the Deseret News was the only newspaper printed in the territory. The editor made a proposition to Aaron Johnson, who was postmaster, that if he would make a monthly payment, a special bulletin of the war news would be sent three times a week. The proposition was read to the usual crowd assembled to hear the news and in a few minutes the amount was raised. It is remembered that E. O. Haymond gave

$5.00 toward the good cause. Three times each week the crowd would gather beneath the box elders that shaded the postoffice door, while the postmaster stood on the steps and read the war news. The names on the mail matter was called off and handed to the person answering "here." In those days but few papers came from the east. Joseph Bissell took Gleason's Literary Companion; Henry Messer, the Cincinnati Times, and some person, whose blessed name is now forgotten, took that precious pictorial paper— Harper's Weekly. These papers were "swiped" from their wrappers by a boy connected with the postoffice, but they were carefully used and returned to their places before called for by the subscribers.

Nicholas Groesbeck purchased the scenery and theatrical properties from the hall at Camp Floyd and built a theater, which, when furnished, was considered the best play house outside of Salt Lake City. That winter some good plays were put on by our local talent, also companies from Salt Lake City and elsewhere. The stage was so constructed that it made a fine dancing floor and it was upon this floor that the first waltz was danced in our town. Henry Walker and James Orton were the chief musicians and introduced a little higher order of music. A bass viol, made and played by Fred Weight and a dulcimer, made by Henry Clegg, were something new and wonderful to those under twenty years of age. And thus passed the 13th year of the settlement of Springville.

The year of 1862 marked a new era in the history of our growing city. During the winter it snowed and rained almost incessantly until the snow was pilled up very deep in the mountains and even in the valley as late as May 1st. All the ravines were filled with snow and when the spring sun began to warm it up the lower lands were submerged, especially the farms on the creek banks, and the lake rose eight feet, reaching up to Dry creek. About the 10th of June the flood reached the climax and began to recede, but it was not until the Fourth of July that the creek could be forded with safety. The first ford was in front of Catherine Boyer's home, where the waters had spread out almost a block. After the flood water was plentiful and the inhabitants began to reach out and increase their holdings.

CHAPTER XIV.

IN the summer of 1863 a company was called to go and meet Brigham Young and party, who were returning from a southern tour. They were coming from Fairview, through Spanish Fork canyon, and as the natives had lately shown signs of unfriendliness it was deemed wise, by the authorities, to send an escort out. Captain Bringhurst's company went up to Thistle and camped over night, with a strong guard posted, and where the author and a number of our boys did their first outpost duty. The next day the President rolled into camp escorted by a party of mounted riflemen from Fairview, who returned home from that point. At the mouth of Spanish Fork canyon the party turned aside for an hour, to watch a race on the two-mile circular race track, which had been prepared by Elmer Taylor and the local sporting men. The party reached town early in the afternoon and the president held a meeting in the evening. In those early days it was the custom to meet President Young and escort him from town to town, where he usually remained for a few days, held meetings and visited the people. During this year, Mathew Caldwell and son were arrested and charged with complicity in the robbery of the United States mail. The overland mail had been attacked near the point of the mountain by a band of Indians, supposedly under the command of Black Hawk. The attack took place just before daylight and the driver, Wood Reynolds, and a United States soldier were killed. The Indians captured the coach animals and the soldier's horse and with parts of the harness and a stolen sabre were seen passing through Springville about 8 o'clock a. m., making for Spanish Fork canyon. They robbed the driver of his purse and watch and this watch was purchased by one of Caldwell's sons, he not knowing, at the time, how the Indian had obtained it. When the watch was identified, sometime afterward, a writ was issued for young Caldwell's arrest for complicity in the crime, and upon the officer attempting to make the arrest, Mathew Caldwell interfered to the extent of resisting a United States officer and a posse went to Sanpete to arrest the father and son. They were brought to Springville, and arriving late, camped in Johnson's lot. Mathew Caldwell and Bishop Johnson were bosom friends, having crossed the plains together in 1850. The Bishop at once planned to rescue his old friend and in furtherance of this plan, he hastily called together a few men whom he could trust and imparted to them the scheme, which was as follows: A fine party was to be hurriedly arranged in the Groesbeck hall to which Major Hempstead and his officers were to be invited. Persons were sent to every part of the town to bring the people together. About 9 o'clock p. m. all the fashion and beauty were assembled,

when the officers together with their
prisoners were ushered into the hall.
The ladies were especially instructed
to use their wiles to so beguile the officers as to make them forget their
prisoners, thereby giving them the opportunity to take "leg bail," which
they proceeded to do about midnight.
The prisoners made their leap for liberty out of a south window, and all the
men made a rush as if to capture the
runaways and the major exclaimed,
"five hundred dollars for the capture of
the prisoners, dead or a live!" They
were never captured. A few days after
the killing of the driver, a battalion of
United States dragoons passed through
our city in quest of the Indians whom
they encountered a few miles beyond
the mouth of Spanish Fork canyon and
were ambushed by them, several soldiers being wounded, one dying the
next day in Springvile, where the soldiers were encamped on a vacant lot.
The Indians received a good drubbing,
however, several being killed and
the rest were put to flight. The
troop had several howitzers mounted
on the backs of mules and when the
grape and canister went screaming into the thickets, the warriers fled in
consternation. The soldiers displayed
several scalps as trophies.

This season there was an effort made
to build an overland mail route to Den-
ver through Hobble creek canyon, into
and through Strawberry valley. A
battalion of United States dragoons
were ordered to march by that route
and they assisted in the construction.
A large contingent of Springville boys
were employed, under the supervision
of Lyman S. Wood. Levi Curtis built
the first station in Hobble creek canyon, just above the Bartholomew fork.
The road went up the left hand fork
and over the first and second Soldier
benches; along the base of Strawberry
peak; thence along the divide into
Strawberry valley. The troops followed with their supply train and per-

REV. GEORGE W. LEONARD

formed about five hours labor daily.
Here our youthful highway builders
heard the tuneful bugler, for the first
time, at reveille and taps, who made the
mountains ring with the martial
strains, morning and evening. It was
about this time that Lieutenant L. J.
Whitney built a sawmill in Strawberry
valley and came to live in Springville.
This year Wm. Bringhurst, L. S.
Wood and Wm. J. Stewart built the
cotton factory at Spring creek, which
is now owned and operated by James
Whitehead, who has had charge since
1880. Under his supervision a large
amount of machinery for woolen work
has been put in and a vast amount of
woolen goods and stocking yarn has
been manufactured. When the factory
was first built, Houtz & Bringhurst
bought the cotton in Washington county, Utah, paying therefor with merchandise and manufactured articles.
The cotton yarn entered extensively
into the home-made clothes for home
use, and was a great saving of labor
which had been formerly performed by
the skilful wives and daughters. John

BOYER HOTEL. P. H. BOYER. PROP'R.

S. Boyer and Jacob Houtz. jr. were agents for the factory. making monthly trips to the cotton country in the interest of the institution.

It was about this period that the modern harvesters and mowers were introduced into our locality. Previous to this time. the old cradle with its crooked snath, one nib and five fingers. propelled by human muscle, had been the harvester. It was a tiresome job for a good man to lay down one acre of grass or two acres of grain in ten hours with the old-fashioned harvesters and mowers. An occasional sewing machine also began to make its appearance to lighten the labors of our woman folk.

A high school was taught this winter in the Big school house by Lyman S. Wood and Wm. Reid. The house was furnished with private desks and seats, by the students. A blackboard graced the western wall where the pupils worked the problems in square root and proportion and diagramed their grammar lessons.

The legislature of 1862-3 amended our city charter. It was found that the larger our city became the less number of officers it took to look after its welfare. In the autumn of 1863 Lyman S. Wood was elected mayor. Wm. J. Stewart. Arba L. Lambson, as aldermen. Moses Childs. Uriah E. Curtis and Lorenzo Johnson as councilors. F. C. Boyer. recorder. Elmer Taylor. marshal. Wm. Bromley was appointed marshal. vice Taylor. resigned March 24, 1864.

Beginning with 1862 Springville sent three teams to the Missouri river to bring out the poor Saints to Utah. These teams continued to go each year until 1868, when the Union Pacific railroad reached Ogden. On some of these trips as many as ten teams were sent. which proved a heavy tax on the people. The wagon train was made up by donation. each furnishing some one thing necessary. such as an ox. wagon. yoke. etc. All donors were given credit on labor tithing for the use of the property or supplies consumed. Generally a couple of beeves were sent from each settlement with the teams. to be slaughtered by the way for food. A night guard was furnished for each ten wagons. whose duty it was to patrol the camp at night. to prevent the dread warriors of the plains from making an attack and stampeding the stock in the darkness. The redskins. all through the sixties. were on the constant lookout for plunder. and it was by the utmost vigilance that the trains returned in safety. John Waters drove one of the first teams that went from Springville and Aaron Johnson jr. was the first night guard. The teamsters were selected by the authorities and outfitted by the ward with all the necessary accouterments. a gun and revolver. clothing and food. Many of our young men. whose names cannot be recalled responded with alacrity to the call. Thus the years 1863-4-5 passed peacefully. nothing occurring to disturb the equanimity of the people in their quiet avocations.

During the years 1864-5. William Dallin was engaged in taking individual orders for merchandise from the people. to be delivered in the autumn of the year. People desiring articles from the east would turn over to him wheat. cattle or horses. for which he found a cash market and the money was sent to his agents in New York. who made the purchases and forwarded the goods to Missouri river points. This freight was transported by wagons. mules and oxen. purchased at these places. to Utah and delivered to the customers. Thos. Dallin and A. G. Sutherland were agents for Wm. Dallin in 1864 and the former went across the plains in 1865 with a company of Mormon missionaries.

from Salt Lake City. who were bound for Europe and various parts of the United States. Mr. Dallin would take the beef cattle. flour and other produce to Montana points in the spring. where he generally found a cash market. receiving as much as $24 per hundred for flour. With this money he made his purchases in the eastern markets. of plows. stoves. groceries. wagons and other articles for his home customers. This scheme worked well for a couple of years. when disaster overtook Mr. Dallin. by the decline of the price of flour in the Montana markets. In 1865 he launched all his own money and all he could get subscribed into the undertaking. but when he reached Montana flour took a fall to such an extent that he was compelled to sell for less than he had given at home. He labored for several years to retrieve his fortunes. but failed and as a consequence. many people suffered loss with him.

In 1865 a contract was let to Solomon D. Chase and John Metcalf to re-model the Big school house into a meeting house for religious worship and the price to be paid was $18.000. The building was finished in the autumn of 1867 and put in its present shape. The actual cost of the meeting house from 1853 to 1867. as compiled from Bishop Johnson's dairy. was: Little school house. the annex to the Big school house. $3000; first cost of the Big school house. $15.000; paid Chase & Metcalf for finishing same. $1700; paid Chase & Metcalf for re-modeling same. $18.000; for fencing and fixtures. $1000. The organ. chandeliers and other furnishings were donated by the people. under the immediate supervision of William Bramall.

In the spring of 1866 the Black Hawk war broke out. which kept our settlement in a ferment of excitement for two years.

Early in May a courier came dashing into town saying that some of our people had been shot at near the forks of the canyon. Immediately the old bell rang out the alarm accompanied by the bass and kettle drums. A rush was made to the meeting house to hear the news. A posse was soon formed under the direction of Bishop Johnson, who was the ranking military officer. Guns and ammunition were quickly prepared and soon twenty men were off for the scene of disturbance. some on horseback and some in wagons. with Captain F. P. Whitmore. who was in command. The scene of the shooting was soon reached. but no dead were found. All the afternoon the mountains were searched for the red marauders. but only a few signs were discovered. About sundown the tired scouts. now re-enforced to thirty in number. gathered at Levi Curtis' ranch where a council of war was held. The conclusion was that the redskins had concealed themselves during the day and after dark would probably take the old Indian trail along the side of the mountain: up the Bartholomew canyon: across Thornton's bench and down into the main canyon near the mouth of Berryport and proceed over into Strawberry valley and thus escape. Figuring on this as a certainty. it was decided that when it became dark, to take ten of the most intrepid men and silently make their way up to Berryport to intercept the savages by ambush. Volunteers were called for and ten responded. Captain Whitmore led the way. Slowly and stealthily the little band followed the road up the canyon. There was no sound except the rush of the water. over its winding way: the occasional howl of a wolf or the scream of a night bird. suddenly disturbed on its perch by the passing scouts. About 10 o'clock p. m. the place of ambush was reached. It seemed fitted by nature for a place to surprise an enemy. On the north was the bare side hill where the trail came down into the canyon. while five or six rods away

were some large clumps of willows whose deep shadows entirely concealed the persons beneath their branches. from which point the trail could be plainly seen. The party was divided into couples for guard duty. when it was discovered that one of the men was missing. He had been seen last by one of the boys while crossing Whitmore creek. It was concluded that he would come in shortly or that he had returned to the Curtis ranch. Two guards were mounted with instructions to quietly awaken the squad. if they should see the Indians coming along the trail. The remainder lay down upon their blankets to slumber. expecting surely to be called before morning to pour a volley into the on-coming redmen. Some time before the first guard was relieved. the youthful Indian hunters were brought to their knees by a fusilade of shots and a blood curdling yell from the guard: "My God. boys! quick! here they come!" Every man felt as though there were a thousand of the enemy in sight. for a moment, but they were as steady as veterans with guns leveled at the darkened trail.. In a moment all was as silent as the grave: not an enemy in sight and it was thought they had taken to cover and would be heard from later. After a moment of awful suspense. the guard explained in whispers. that they had seen a band of five or six Indians appear on the trail about fifty yards away. and had concluded. after a short consultation. to fire into them which would also awaken their comrades. Nothing was seen or heard. however. but a more vigilant watch was kept until morning.

When daylight came the trail was examined. but the trail being very hard at this point no tracks were discernable and whether there had been Indians present. or whether the "bogie man" took possession of the imagination of the youthful guards was never known. However. the actual experience of the boys was as real as though the enemy had been in sight. The trailers descended the canyon to the ranch in the early morning and found the missing scout eating breakfast with the boys. He had stopped to get a drink and becoming turned around in the windings of the ford, had come out on the wrong side of the creek, and being thus bewildered, did not realize that he was going down the canyon until he found himself at his former starting place. Provisions had been forwarded to the party the evening previous and the boys had killed a stray sheep from which the tired and hungry boys, who had not tasted food since the morning before, made a splendid meal. Then they started for home, looking carefully for signs all the way. At the first bridge fresh moccasin tracks were discovered, crossing the road, toward the Union bench and thence up the Spanish Fork canyon.

Once during the summer Indians were seen though a glass hovering about Kolob, and as there was stock in that vicinity, a platoon of minute men was hastily summoned and sent to scale the heights and capture the braves; kill them or drive them away. As the boys left Bishop Johnson said: "Bring their scalps." The boys went up and brought the stock safely down, without "raising any hair." for not an Indian was seen though some of the boys declared that they had seen moccasin tracks.

CHAPTER XV.

ALL summer and autumn parties went for wood, thirty or forty in number, well armed, as a protection against their wily foe. Pickets were stationed at the mouth of the canyon and lookouts in the tower to see the fire signals agreed upon. Often in the night the old bell awakened the people from their slumbers, indicating that the painted warrior was hovering near. A company of minute men was organized under command of Captain Jesse Steele, that camped in the tithing yard for six months. The company was well mounted and armed and slept upon their weapons every night ready to answer the call of the bell or martial drum or fife. Each day a squad was detailed to go out with the cow herd which was driven upon the Union bench. The pickets patrolled the foothills all day to look out for the enemy and in case of a signal from the canyon to rush the cattle home in short order. A detail was made each morning to cut forage in the city pasture for the horses' feed at night. At dusk the minute men assembled at the barracks for roll call, after which they lay down to sleep under the shade of the apple trees with the green sward for a couch. The evening was spent in story telling, singing and games. The genial Dougall; the loquacious Holley, excitable Messer, fun-loving Tunbridge, and jocular Geo. McKinzie, are well remembered and familiar figures of the troop. The boys, just doing their first scouting and real service as Indian fighters, were represented by John W. Deal, jr., M. E. Crandall, Joseph Bringhurst, Leroy Bird and D. C. Johnson.

During the summer a requisition was sent from General Wells to General Johnson for a contingent from Springville to go into Sanpete county to help defend the settlers from the attacks of the Indians. It was in Sanpete and Sevier valleys where the Indians made

made their most formidable attacks. About forty of our stalwarts were called for this important service. All who could not outfit themselves were assisted by the members of the ward. Wm. Bramall aided as commissary, and most of the supplies were sent through his orders. He, Colonel Bromley and Thomas Child did much arduous and praiseworthy work in raising and forwarding supplies to the front and assisting the families of the home soldiers.

At three different times during the summer did some of the Springville boys distinguish themselves by being under fire and hearing the blood-curdling warwhoops of the painted heathen Wm. Tunbridge and W. L. Johnson, then a lad of sixteen, and W. I. Hall, were at the fight at Gravelly ford, under General Pace, where the former was shot through the leg. John H. Noakes, Elial Curtis and Del Stewart also had a hair-breadth escape while carrying the express from Gunnison to Glen Cove, early in June. In that day

three or four men, well mounted, were sent upon express duty, the work was so hazardous. The boys started out and rode gayly along for about fifteen miles without seeing any hostile demonstration. Suddenly as they were passing a point near the Gravelly ford they were fired upon by ten painted demons. None of the couriers were hit, however, and they put spurs to their steeds and rode like the wind for the Glen with the howling horde in hot pursuit. Noakes and Stewart were superbly mounted, but Curtis' horse, early in the race, began to show symptoms of distress and fell behind. His companions slackened their speed to keep pace with their slower comrade and the enemy gained steadily and were getting uncomfortably close, when Noakes and Stewart leaped from their horses and throwing their guns across their saddles fired at the pursuing fiends which caused them to draw rein, while Curtis lashed his pony to the front at its utmost speed. When he

OFFICE OF THE SPRINGVILLE INDEPENDENT

had gained a hundred yards his companions re-mounted and overtook him. These adroit tactics were pursued for several miles until safety was insured. It was an exciting and dangerous race and was carried out with superb coolness and bravery. This same season. over the same route. an express squad was fired upon and Heber Houtz, a former Springville boy. was killed and left upon the field while his three companions saved themselves by out-riding their vengeful pursuers.

The Black Hawk soldiers. who went to Sanpete in 1866 were as follows. being an exact copy from Wm. Bramall's book. A full report will be given to show how the outfits were obtained. as all were a public donation. both as to men and accouterments: Richard Westwood: rifle and sabre, furnished by himself: horse. by John Whitbeck: saddle by Joshua Fielding: bridle by Don Johnson: forty-seven cartridges. by S. C. Perry: eighty cartridges. by Nephi Packard: revolver. by Thomas Roylance. J. T. Lisonbee. horse. saddle. bridle. gun. pistol and 100 rounds of ammunition. furnished by Edward Friel. D. C. Huntington. paid $20 per month for a substitute. Fred Singleton—Ruben Howell furnished the horse: Jas. Oakley. the saddle: Singleton furnished the Yager: J. D. Wood & Son. eighty rounds of ammution. Geo. Richardson —horse. saddle and bridle. furnished by his father: rifle and cartridges. by Wm. Roylance. Moroni Fuller—horse. Cyrus Sanford: saddle. Thos. Snelson: bridle. Jonathan Harrington: Yager. Henry Roylance: ammunition. William Bromley. Allen Lambson—furnished horse, saddle and bridle. pistol and fifty rounds of ammunition: Spencer rifle and ammunition. by Arba L. Lambson. Francis C. Boyer—sent substitute. Jesse Riblin: paid $40 per month—G. D. Wood & Son. furnished horse: saddle. Elial Curtis: bridle. Watson Houtz: gun. Joshua Fielding: sabre. Philip Boyer: pistol and ammunition. John S.

Boyer. Henry Jennings—furnished horse himself: saddle. M. E. Crandall: Joslyn carbine. Wm. J. Stewart: forty-nine rounds of ammunition. Wm. M. Bromley. Samuel Gully—horse. M. P. Crandall: saddle and bridle he furnished himself: Spencer rifle. Sanford Fuller: thirty-five cartridges and sabre. by himself. Walter Wheeler—horse and bridle. M. P. Crandall: saddle. John Maycock: gun. N. H. Groesbeck: forty-one cartridges and sabre. by Robert Watson: revolver and ammunition. Richard Thorne. Wm. L. Johnson—horse. Richard Collins. saddle: G. D. Wood & Son: Ballard rifle. Wm. Hall: pistol. Wm. Lisonbee: ammunition. by Albert Worthen and Wm. Hall: bridle. was furnished by himself. Thomas Brown—horse. saddle and bridle. by Jacob Houtz: Smith & Wesson rifle and ammunition. S. C. Perry. Daniel Alleman—horse. saddle and bridle. by himself: Sharp's rifle. 200 caps. nineteen balls. ten cartridges. H. M. Dougall: pistol. 100 rounds of ammunition. himself. Samuel Tew—rifle Andrew Wild: 1½ pounds of lead. Wm. Bromley: one quilt. Sister Wordsworth. One span of mules. harness and wagon. John W. Deal. The latter was used as baggage wagon and thus equipped the boys moved to the front.

There were subsequently called to go to Sanpete in 1866-7. the following citizens. who were fitted up as were the first contingent: F. P. Whitmore. Amos S. Warren. F. Beardall. Geo. Harrison. J. M. Westwood. T. A. Brown. Albert Harmer. Edwin Lee. Elial Curtis. Samuel Bulkley. M. D. Childs. Robt. Kirkman. J. H. Noakes. David Dibble. R. L. Mendenhall. Henry Curtis. Wm. Kerswell, W. I. Hall. John Davis. Thos. Medina: R. L. Mendenhall was lieutenant and Elial Curtis was sergeant: Charley Stevenson. bugler.

On the 27th of June a successful fight took place between a band of Indians and a detachment from Spanish Fork and Springville. On the evening of the 26th a band of Indians came down Maple canyon, made a foray into the valley as far as Roundy's pasture and drove off some fifty horses and twenty head of cattle into Maple canyon. H. M. Dougall and D. E. Deal had been the mounted videttes the previous day and had patrolled the country between Hobble Creek and Spanish Fork canyons. camping with the squad over night at the first bridge in the former canyon. As they rode into town early the next morning they met Bishop Johnson, who asked them if they had seen any Indians. Their reply was: "No. no sign of Indians; everything is all right." The Bishop replied: "No, everything is not all right: the Indians came down Maple canyon last night and took a herd of cattle from Markham's pasture at Spanish Fork, and some horses from Roundy's pasture. Go and tell Colonel Bromley to come quickly." Bromley was summoned, the old bell spoke, the drums beat, and in twenty minutes several of the mounted minute men were on the public square, armed and ready to go. It was about 9 a. m. and a dispatch had been sent to Colonel Creer. of Spanish Fork. to meet the Springville squad at the mouth of Maple canyon. and all proceed under the command of Creer on the trail of the hostiles. to recover the stock if possible. The names of the Springville squad. so far as can be remembered. were: T. L. Mendenhall. Oscar Crandall. Alma Spafford. J. A. Groesbeck. John Edmundson. Loren Dibble. D. C. Johnson. and an old soldier by the name of Gillespie. The other members of the minute company were in the fields and could not be reached in time. A gallop of thirty minutes brought the young troopers to the mouth of the canyon. but by the indications Creer's men had arrived first and gone on up the canyon. Our boys rode rapidly after them. mile after mile. until they had crossed the divide

and descended the steep trail into the head of Diamond Fork, but could see nothing of the Spanish Fork troopers. There were three young mad-caps in the squad that day, who kept riding ahead in their anxiety to find the Indians. When the party came to within a half mile of the spot where the skirmish took place the three boys, who were still ahead, rode up on a knoll and gave a whoop, for a little way in advance they could see Creer's men under a clump of trees and firing over toward the south side of the broad flat canyon. With a yell the advance guard charged toward their white friends, followed by the boys in the rear. Just as the three mad-caps got within a hundred yards of the party they were suddenly fired upon by a number of Indians who, at that moment, were in the act of flanking the Spanish Fork boys. They had found their Indians, but instead of engaging them in a hand to hand combat Dibble turned to the right and came back to the main body; Groesbeck was unhorsed by the breaking of his saddle girth, but he clung to the halter strap as his horse circled to the left and back to his comrades in the rear. Edmundson kept straight ahead and to the left of the Spanish Forkers, until he was lost to view by the intervening brush. The Springville boys quickly dismounted and. leaving their horses with one of the men. advanced cautiously toward Creer's command. At this juncture several Indians were seen to retreat hastily from their position on the south and disappear in the thicket which hedged Diamond creek. The Spanish Fork boys had been in their position for an hour and had seen some warm work. Al Dimmick was fatally wounded and lay upon a bed of leaves in the shade.

In a few moments an Indian appeared upon the bluff and by his excited gestures seemed to be haranguing his men. Some shots were exchanged, but the effect was not known as both sides were laying low. Presently Colonel Creer selected five long range rifles and began volley firing at the chief, some 800 yards distant, and at about the fifth volley the Indian fell upon the neck of his horse, which ran behind the hill and out of sight. The Indians were then seen scampering over the ridge, and were variously estimated at from twenty to fifty. All was quiet for the next half hour and a careful scout was made, but no sign of the enemy was visible and it was concluded that they had drawn off with their dead and wounded and would renew the attack after nightfall. Feeling sure of a night attack, a courier was sent to town for help. The man who volunteered to undertake this perilous task was the old veteran, Gillespie. It was 4 p. m. when he departed, reaching town about 7 o'clock with news of the fight, the extreme peril of the white men and that Edmundson was missing. The tocsin bell, in quick, sharp tones brought the minute men from their quarters and by 8 p. m. they had started under the direction of the scout to relieve their companions from their extreme peril.

In the meantime the Indian camp, which had been abandoned at the beginning of the attack by the whites with all it contained, was relieved by the Spanish Fork contingent of the butcher knives, new hats, bridles and lariats which the enemy had left in his flight. One man had nine new army hats, and the others each had some trophy. Poor Dimmick was tenderly placed upon a litter and just after sunset the party started on their return home, expecting at any moment to hear the crack of the deadly rifle and the piercing warwhoop. They were compelled to carry their wounded comrade, who groaned in agony at every step. At times he entreated his bearers to kill him and end his sufferings. Tirelessly the troop ascended the east-

ern slope of the mountain out of the Diamond, winding up the precipitous and hazardous mountain trail. The front and rear guards kept keenly on the alert, in order to prevent an ambush. About midnight the pass was reached and the descent upon the home side of the mountain began. Near the summit the relief party was met and not until then did the returning party realize that it was safe. Still slowly the homeward journey was continued and completed just at daybreak.

In front of the old hall they were met by Bishop Johnson, who praised the boys for their good work, told them to get a few hours sleep and at the call of the bell to assemble for the purpose of returning to the scene of the fight to search for Edmundson, who had not returned. It was thought he had escaped and would perhaps reach home through some of the canyon passes. Alas! vain hope! The poor boy lay upon the lonely hillside cold in death, with the moon beams shining in his up-turned face.

At 7 p. m. the loud alarm bell called the weary troopers from their blankets and in a very few moments they were on the march, under the command of Captain Steele. At the mouth of Maple canyon they found Colonel Creer, with his company. This morning they had deemed it advisable to wait for the Springville contingent. Under the command of Colonel Creer the party proceeded to the scene of the combat of the previous day, arriving without incident. They found the camp intact, the enemy not having returned for his camp equipage. There were seventeen saddles by actual count, and other horse trappings used by the native rider, but no other appearance of an enemy. The day before the hostiles had killed two or three beeves, and large flitches of the juicy steaks still hung upon the rocks and brush where the thieves had placed them to sun-dry. The horses were left under the guard of a part of the troop, while the others in squads trailed the mits in every direction in search of traces of the missing man. After a toilsome search and just about sundown his mangled body was found three-fourths of a mile north of the battle ground. He had been stripped of his shirt, his right hand was severed at the wrist, his scalp torn off and the savage foe had shot him twice through the heart, the muzzle of the weapon being held so close that the body was powder-burned. A signal gun was fired to notify the searchers that the hunt was ended, and all gathered quickly to their horses. When the boys came in they brought some of the stolen stock, among which was a horse belonging to Wm. Smith with blood stains upon the withers and down the front leg—the animal supposed to have been ridden by the war-chief the previous day. The dead man was placed upon this horse by Thomas Dallin and then came a discussion as to whether the company should return

home via Spanish Fork canyon, there being a good wagon road all the way, or take trail back through Maple canyon. It was eventually decided to take the back trail and the bugle sounded the advance. At this juncture the horse with the dead rider began to buck and rear and plunge in a fearful manner and could not be quieted. It was held for a moment while the body could be removed and strapped upon the back of "Old Beck," a family mare belonging to William Mendenhall and Richard Mendenhall mounted the refractory broncho and the march homeward was commenced and was finished at 3 a. m. and the dead man was placed upon a bier in front of the old hall, when the now thoroughly fatigued rough riders went to rest. Hardly had their tired heads sank upon their pillows when the signal (three quick flashes) was made at the mouth of Spanish Fork canyon and seen by the guard in the tower and the bell from its iron throat rang out, "Come! Come! Come. Quick! Quick! Quick!" A few of the tired riders rallied, also some of the citizens in wagons, drove like Jehu to the mouth of Spanish Fork canyon and surprised the guard there by their sudden and warlike appearance. The guard said they had seen Indians appear some distance up the canyon and had made one light (be upon your guard), but as it had been only a flash, and fearing the lookout hadn't seen it, another handful of brush had been thrown on the fire, which only emitted a faint flash, when a larger amount had been put upon the embers and a satisfactory blaze kindled. The watchmen had seen all three of the flashes and acted accordingly. After scouring the vicinity of the mouth of the canyon where fresh Indian signs were plainly seen, the cavalcade returned home. Thus ended three very exciting days. Some of the boys had been forty-eight hours in the saddle, almost without food or sleep.

The Diamond fight was the most successful engagement of the war in this: That the Indians were thoroughly whipped, their entire camp equipage falling into the hands of the victors, who also brought back some of the horses and all of the cattle except those killed. A report came from Duchesne not long afterward, that the dusky marauders had eight killed and wounded, and that Black Hawk was the rider who left his blood-stains upon the captured horse. On the day after the return of the expedition, Dimmick and Edmundson were buried with military honors. Thus ended the fight upon the Diamond, which was also the end of the Indian hostilities in our vicinity.

CHAPTER XVI.

ABOUT the 1st of July, 1866, while Sheppard's singing class was in the bowery practicing songs for the annual celebration a thunder storm came up suddenly and one of the bolts fell so near Wm. Mendenhall that he was stricken down and for some time was thought to be fatally injured. He rallied, however, and after many days fully recovered. This singing class created a great furore for a time. Mr. Sheppard, a recent comer from Southampton, England, came to live at Springville and, being an enthusiast in the Tonic Sol Fa system, he had during the previous winter organized a class of over seventy-five pupils who attained quite a proficiency in singing exercises. Wm. Mendenhall was one of his patrons and took a great interest in the class.

On the Diamond expedition acres of dry poles had been discovered on a large flat near the summit of Maple canyon. These trees had been fire-killed and were just right for poles, "straight as candles and as dry as a bone. Later in the season hundreds of loads were brought out for fencing and fuel. And such loads as were brought out by the boys, each of whom tried to excel his neighbor in the size of his load and the beauty of the poles!

Bishop Johnson built, this year, upon his own lot and at his own expense, a school house, and fitted it up with a sort of desk not unlike the patent desk of today—in fact, made upon the same principle, less the 'finish and polish. The reason for this was, the school houses were not keeping up with the growth of the children demanding school facilities. Oliver B. Huntington was installed as principal, and D. C. Johnson as his assistant. By this time school books were becoming more plentiful, but as yet were of many kinds and very costly. Pencils cost 25 cents each, or five for $1, and everything else in proportion.

C. D. Evans taught school in the "little school house" during the winter. It may be said in this connection that Mr. Evans was the first teacher to come to Springville (arriving in 1858) who was able to teach the higher branches, and who first awakened in the breasts of our youth a desire for higher polish and discovered to them the possibilities of a higher education. He brought to our schools a system of grammar wholly new to the majority of the boys, who had formerly only a crude idea of the parts of speech—"mountain grammar" being the only code. He also introduced the higher mathematics. Heretofore to master the common branches was the highest ambition of the average schoolboy. Many a boy and girl took a new inspiration from Prof. Evans and will always cherish his memory as the real pioneer educator of Springville of the higher type.

The municipal election of 1867 resulted in the selection of Cyrus Sanford as mayor; R Richard Bird and Wm. P. Johnson as aldermen: Francis C. Boyer, Osias Strong and Wm. Robinson, councilors; F. C. Boyer as recorder;

RESIDENCE OF LYMAN S. WOOD, BUILT IN 1862.

and William M. Bromley as marshal.

During this summer it was reported by the guards at the mouth of Hobble Creek canyon that they had seen several fresh Indians tracks leading into the valley. The intelligence was communicated to Gen. Johnson, who concluded that the thieves had secreted themselves among the willows in the west field with the intention of stealing horses the following night and escaping into the canyon. To prevent such a scheme being carried out a party of scouts were sent, just as soon as night had fallen, up into the canyon to mount guard at the second bridge and intercept the thieves in case they came that way. They were to go and remain over one day, returning the second night before daylight. The party consisted of B. T. Blanchard, who was in command, Henry Messer, John R. Miller, John W. Deal, jr., John A. Groesbeck, M. E. Crandall and D. C. Johnson. The scouting party went up through the fields along Hobble creek to the place designated and kept a close watch through the night. During the day they lay close beneath a high bank near the second bridge, one of the party remaining on guard while the others slept. The day was thus spent until dark, when one of the guard came down to the camp in great haste and excitement and reported that there was an Indian just up by the Packard dugway, mounted, and that he had got a good view of one through an opening in the brush, and that there were evidently several others.

The boys quickly ascended to the road and hastily arranged themselves on each side, with instructions to allow the enemy to get between and then fire. By this time the clatter of horses' hoofs were plainly discernable, and the hearts of the youthful Indian hunters were thumping within their jackets. Closer and closer came the sound, when in a sudden turn in the road there came in full view, not an Indian in warpaint and feathers, but old Abraham Perdue, a person well known to all the boys! All stepped into the road in front of the rider and he, surprised in his turn, threw up his hands and exclaimed, "Don't shoot!" He had been over to the reservation at Duchesne on some mission pertaining to Indian affairs. Perdue was permitted to proceed, when he perhaps should have been detained, as the circumstance of his appearance at that time and place would have seemed to older persons to be at least a little suspicious. There was no sleeping that night, but the squad kept close together and proceeded quietly by stages down to the mouth of the canyon, reporting just before daylight at headquarters to the effect that its expedition had been bootless.

About the New Year a great gold excitement prevailed that awakened our little town to an extent never before known except in the Indian wars. Gold had been found in rich abundance, so it was alleged, at the mouth of Pole Haven. It had been kept a profound secret for some weeks by a prospector, but had leaked out and set the town all agog with excitement. Nearly every man and boy in the city rushed madly away for the "diggings" to make a fortune. They left by day, they rushed off by night. One morning at 9 a. m. when the junior teacher came to the school house he found a note on his desk informing him that the senior teacher had "skipped by the light of the moon" for the region of the gold camp and asking him to do the best he could with the school, adding that his name would be recorded upon a good claim. Excitement was high; everybody had "gold in his eye." Bishop Miller came over from Provo, got Bishop Johnson and up the canyon they went as fast as the nimble-footed mules would travel. When the two ecclesiastics reached "Eagle City" three rousing cheers went up, as now the prospectors felt that they had full authority to dig and delve for the hidden treasure. Claims were paced off—there was no time for the slow Gunter's chain. A city was staked off and town lots chosen. Soon after the arrival of the Bishops some of the more sagacious discovered the scent of the traditional mouse. No gold nor color could be found and it finally leaked out that the ground had been "salted" with some of the rich rock brought in by the gold hunters from the Sweetwater mines the previous spring. Slowly the fever

THOMAS CHILD

abated and the disgusted people returned to their homes, to joke and laugh the remainder of the winter about the many ludicrous incidents which had occurred. There is a tradition extant that the only persons who made anything out of the affair were H. M. Dougall, who was recorder of the district and collected some of his fees in advance, and James Holley, who gathered up a couple of loads of stakes which made good kindling wood.

In the autumn of 1866 the Deseret telegraph line was projected, and completed during the following autumn. The line was built by subscription. The people of Springville built six miles of line, furnishing wire, poles and labor to set them; also their pro rata of cash to buy instruments. Men went to the canyon after poles and delivered them along the line, where others set them in the ground. Wm. Bryan of Nephi was the first operator at Springville, but after some weeks he was superceded by Miss Belvidera Parks, also of Nephi. About this time

Brigham Young sent out a circular to the Bishops. asking them to select a few young men and women to learn telegraphy. They were to regard it as a mission. One of the cards was hung up. and read something as follows:

"The operators are to regard themselves as missionaries, who spend their time without compensation."

Some of the early operators did this. but they ultimately received some pay: in some cases from the city through the tithing office and by private subscription. Those called from Springville to learn telegraphy were: D. C. Johnson. Lydia M. Boyer. Elizabeth Mendenhall and Adelaide Huntington. The two former were employed in the home office, Spanish Fork. Nephi. Eureka and Tintic.

Ever since 1861 Spicer W. Crandall, Noah Guyman and Dorr P. Curtis. had acted as counselors to Bishop Johnson. Guyman had moved from Springville and as the Bishop was entitled to two counselors. on account of his bishopric.

and presidency of the Branch, he called some of the leading ecclesiastics to meet at his counsel chamber, to make the selection to fill the vacant places. Some twenty was present and it was proposed to make the selection by ballot. Slips of paper was passed to each person, who wrote a name there, and then put the paper in a hat. When the ballots were counted Wm. Bramall and Wm. Bromley were found to have the greatest number of votes and were declared the chosen ones. They remained in that position until the time of the resignation of the Bishop.

In 1867 the grasshoppers again made their appearance and did much damage. The autumn previous they had deposited their eggs in all that area known as the clay beds. When they hatched in the spring and before they could fly they commenced their migration toward several hundred acres of wheat on Dry creek and its destruction was imminent unless some barrier was interposed to stop them. Bishop John-

SPRINGVILLE BANKING COMPANY'S BUILDING. BUILT IN 1892.

son called upon
all the people
to turn out and
dig a ditch two
miles long be-
tween the hun-
gry horde and
the waving
grain. This
ditch was three
feet wide at the
top, four feet
on the bottom
and three feet
deep. Sunday
was the day, as
the danger was
imminent and
the army of
"iron-clads"
had no regard
for the Sab-

RESIDENCE OF JUDGE JOHN S. BOYER.

bath, but kept travelling grimly on
and by Monday it would have been too
late. Every able-bodied man and boy
with pick, spade and grubbing hoe
turned out. The mothers and daughters went along with baskets full of
picnic for the noon-day repast. Indeed, it was partly a holiday, and the
good work was accomplished and
proved effectual. The invading army
moved into the pit that had been dug,
loose dirt was thrown upon them and
the people saved their grain.

About August 1st. 1867, the first
Young Men's Improvement Society was
organized in Springville. It happened
in this wise. In the afternoon of the
24th of July, Wm. M. Bromley, A. G.
Sutherland, John S., P. H. and F. C.
Boyer and D. C. Johnson, met socially
under the bowery while the dance was
in progress and the propriety of organizing an educational society was discussed. It was agreed to meet at Colonel Bromley's a few evenings later to
talk further about the matter and per-
fect an organizaton. This was done
and the society completed by electing
A. G. Sutherland as president, Wm.

Bromley vice-president, and F. C.
Boyer, secretary. Weekly meetings
were held at the various residences in
town during the autumn, and in the
winter a few more names were added.
The admission fee was $1.00 per year,
payable in advance. The object was
educational. At the meetings parlia-
mentary rules were observed. When a
member arose to declaim or read and
had finished, a friendly criticism was indulged in. If grammatical errors were
made or wrong positions taken, or im-
proper gestures used, they were pointed
out, oftimes causing a lively debate as
to the correctness of the criticism. During the winter Prof. C. D. Evans was
made a member of the society, by request, also Thos. Child and others.
There was no solicitation for members,
but those of good moral character who
applied for membership were admitted.
The members used their utmost endeavor to make the society a desirable
one and members came pouring in,
each gladly paying the initiation fee
of $1.00. During the winter the mem-
bership grew until fifty had been
added. The money was spent for

books which were well read by the members. During the season Prof. Evans gave a series of grammar lessons with full attendance. Within two years the membership increased to 100. Annual elections were held and during the existance of the society, Wm. Bromley, F. C. Boyer and D. C. Johnson acted as presidents. This society lasted until the winter of 1875, when it was merged into the general M. I. A. movement, under the auspices of the church of L. D. S. Those now remembered as active officers and workers in the society were: James E. Hall, Aaron Johnson, W. H. Carter, H. M. Dougall, John S. Boyer, P. H. Boyer and Abram

Noe. John Carter built a little frame building as a private study which he furnished as a library, and he acted as librarian for most of the time and issued books to the members. One year the membership reached 140 and the number of books in the library were 260. Weekly meetings were held in the meeting house, during the winter months, that were crowded because of the excellent programs.

Cyrus E. Dallin, our sculptor boy, while in Springville in 1900, spoke of the little library, kept by John Carter, where, as a lad, he imbibed much of his love for literature and learning. Some of those books which composed that

STORE BUILDING OF DEAL BROS. & MENDENHALL

library are now in the possession of some of our people and are highly prized by the owners, for it was in the life of this library that many of our young men indulged fully their desire for reading for the first time.

In 1868 our town sent its quota of teams after the poor—this year, ten teams, with four yoke of oxen in each. Two night guards were also sent—E. A. Clark, with the Springville teams under Captain Holman. of Pleasant Grove, and D. C. Johnson accompanied the "Dixie" train, under Captain Daniel McArthur. They were long, arduous trips, fraught with danger for man and beast. The long, plodding journey, monotonous from day to day; ferrying and swimming rivers; the picket guard at night, to constantly keep watch against the marauders of the plains; the stampedes and night alarms, made the trip one of constant danger. This year, two days before Captain McArthur's train crossed Green river, which was raging and above its natural banks, the Sanpete train while ferrying the angry flood lost nine of their young men by the capsizing of the ferry boat. Coming back the journey was more interesting for some of the boys. McArthur's train was enlivened by an army of girls, emigrating that year from some of the large cities of England. Some of the boys secured partners for the journey of life from among the fair damsels, on the voyage over the plains to Zion.

It may not be out of place here to notice how the teams, outfits and men were secured for these expeditions, going yearly after the poor. From 1861 to 1868, Springville sent her full share of teams and men. A good idea of how these trains were equipped and made up for the arduous journey can be fully appreciated by quoting from the minutes of a teacher's meeting, held on March 23rd, 1868, wherein Spicer W. Crandall presided and John M. Clements was clerk. A selection of teams,

teamsters. etc.. had been made at a meeting held previously at the Bishop's house, where teachers had been appointed to see the brethren and report at the next meeting whether they would "respond to the call" or not. The report was as follows:

"Thomas Roylance did not know what he could do as yet. Bro. Philo Dibble had gone to the mines. Hugh M. Dougall was heavily in debt and could not furnish the mules, but would furnish a wagon. Wm. Sumsion would furnish one span of mules. Loren Roundy was not able to furnish horses, but would furnish a yoke of oxen. W. J. Stewart would furnish one span of mules and harness complete. E. Stewart, if he didn't trade his mules off, would send a span. E. O. Haymond, jr., would not send his mules unless they were secured to him. Chas. Allen and Joseph Hewlet would go as teamsters. The Spafford Bros. needed all the mules they had. but would send one yoke of oxen. Mart Taylor would furnish one span of mules. Oscar Crandall could not furnish a span of mules, but would furnish one yoke of oxen. Augustus Durfee would go as a teamster. Edward Friel would furnish one yoke of oxen. John Roylance would pay for the hire of one span of mules or one yoke of oxen."

The minutes of the teachers' meetings. kept by Joseph D. Reynolds. give many other items. as, "Wood & Bringhurst are assessed $50 mdse. to help fit out the teamsters to go after the poor," N. H. Groesbeck $50 and Wm. J. Stewart $25. And most vigorous protests are entered by those same merchants against the large assessments.

In 1868 the Relief Society was organized under the presidency of Mrs. Cynthia Clyde. Mrs. Hannah Harrison and Mary Ann Roylance were appointed as her counselors, and Mrs. Mary A. Johnson was secretary. This society has continued in active existence ever since. reaching out its kindly hands to the poor and succoring many in want.

In the spring of this year many of our citizens went to work on Brigham Young's contract upon the Union Pacific Railroad, then as far as Laramie and which was completed to Ogden soon after the New Year. In 1869 many of our contractors went out to

RESIDENCE OF E. J. YARD.

work on the grade of the Central Pacific near and beyond the Promontory. (Many of our Springville railroad men got their first experience as railroad graders in 1868-9.

In the autumn of 1838 the co-operative system was fully launched at the October conference and the parent institution was organized at Salt Lake City. Co-operation was urged by eloquent preachers sent from headquarters all over the state, and talk of "freezing out" was frequently heard f om some of the more enthusiastic promoters of the scheme. At this time N. H. Groesbeck and Wood & Bringhurst were the merchants of the town. Public meetings were called locally and stock subscribed by over three hundred people.

Stock was issued in $5 shares and it was stipulated in the articles of incorporation that no person would be permitted to hold more than $200 in stock in the institution. This latter clause was inserted to prevent monopoly. A "Co-op" store was started in Bishop Johnson's school house, with the Bishop as president. Wm. M. Bromley as superintendent and C. D. Evans as secretary. The sign of the "All-Seeing Eye" and "Holiness to the Lord" were suspended over the portal. The new stock was put in and business commenced. N. H. Groesbeck sold his stock of merchandise to the Co-op at the start and the other merchants followed in a short time.

CHAPTER XVII.

IN the spring of 1868 Cyrus Sanford was re-elected mayor. The aldermen were Wm. Bringhurst and Wm. D. Johnson, with the following councilmen: Osias Strong, F. C. Boyer and John S. Boyer. F. C. Boyer was installed as recorder and Wm. M. Bromley as marshal.

During this summer Dan Costello's circus and menagerie came to our city and gave two performances that delighted the people, especially the younger ones who had never seen a collection of wild animals. The occasion was by mutual consent made a public holiday and nearly every person turned out to see the elephant.

In the autumn Bishop Johnson built another school house, at the corner of Johnson and Main streets. which was also used for dancing and theatricals. F. C. Boyer and D. C. Johnson taught school there the first winter. They had taught the winter previously in the old hall over Thomas Tame's harness shop near the old cottonwood tree. It was at these schools where some of our citizens commenced their rudimentary educational pursuits. Among those well-remembered were H. T. Reynolds. George Sutherland and Clarence Crandall.

A grand military ball was given during the winter, to which were invited the military officials' of Spanish Fork and Provo. The people of our neighboring towns returned the compliment by inviting our military men to like balls. For several years preceding a great interest had been taken in military affairs. Annual encampments had been held. where all the militia of the district had gathered for division drill and general camp duty. These encampments were very popular and well-attended. Hundreds of the inhabitants turned out upon such occasions. which gave additional interest to the drills. These encampments usually continued for three days and wound up with a grand field movement and sham battle. A dress ball was also given by the young ladies of the town. that has never been excelled for variety of costume. splendid character representation and general enjoyment. It was a grand success in every way. Great interest was also taken in sword exercises. An expert fencing master—an Englishman. Captain Martin by name —taught a series of fencing schools in Utah county. calling one day per week at the six principal towns.

He organized a class here of some forty pupils, some of whom became quite expert in the art of fencing. This fencing fad spread all over the state, from Cache valley to Washington county. and many of the citizens—and ladies as well—became quite expert in the use of the small sword. Contests frequently took place between the members of the Springville and Spanish Fork classes, which proved a very pleasant recreation. As usual a ball or two were exchanged between the towns on account of the exercises in swordsmanship.

In 1870 Bishop Johnson resigned his bishopric in consequence of failing health. He had served the people as a father long and faithfully. He was a true friend to the poor and many poor men had been given a start financially upon their arrival in the city for permanent residence. He kept an open house for all travelers and was never known to charge for such accommodations as he could give. Even the Indians, to whom he was an unfailing friend. always found food for man and horse at his house. As many as forty dusky braves have sat at one time at his table. When he was 61 years old he had two dozen photographs of the smaller size taken. upon the backs of which he wrote a conciseautobiography. and gave to some of his nearest friends. This autobiography is here added verbatim:

"Aaron Johnson. born in Hadam, Conn.. June 22. 1806. Joined Methodists. 1820. Joined the Latter-Day Saints in 1836. Ordained an elder at Kirtland. Ohio, in 1837. Ordained a seventy at Farwest. Mo.. in 1838. Ordained a high priest and high counselor at Nauvoo. Ill.. in 1842. Took a mission in 1843. Justice of the peace in Nauvoo. Ill.. for four years. President of Garden Grove. Ill.. in 1846. High counselor at Winter Quarters. Nebraska. in 1847. Took mission. horseback. through Iowa. Illinois. Indiana.

Michigan and Ohio in 1848. Bishop and president of Kanesville and Pottawattomie branch. Iowa. in 1849-50, and went on a mission to New England States in winter of same year. Captain of a Company of 135 wagons across the plains to Salt Lake City in 1850. Judge of Utah county for three years. Bishop and postmaster of Springville for 17 years. High counselor Provo Stake of Zion 17 years. Member of the Legislative assembly 17 years. Delegate to Constitutional convention to draft constitution for State of Deseret. Held three Military commissions under Governor Ford of Illinois. Elected Brigadier General l'etcetneet military district 1857. and commissioned major general in 1866. by Chas. Durkee, Governor of Utah. Now in my 61st year when this picture was taken; have nine wives and forty-eight children. Enjoy the best of health. Still hold the office of Bishop and p stmaster. High Counselor. the several ordin-

ations and Major General, and still look forward and upward.

"A. JOHNSON."

William Bringhurst was ordained Bishop with Wm. H. Kelsey and Solomon D. Chase as counselors. An entire re-organization of the ecclesiastical branch was perfected and new and younger men were called to the various church official positions and everything moved along as of yore. in many respects. though the new Bishop found it necessary to soon call to his aid many of the old officers of the former Bishop.

In the mid-summer the Sunday school people constructed a bowery upon the lake shore. straight down Main street. The Dallin Bros.. John and Thomas. had launched a very fine yacht. of their own construction. which they could handle like true sons of the wave and had promised the people a grand sail whenever they would come down to the lake. The Dallins were expert

THE MANITOU HOTEL. MRS. MOSE JOHNSON. PROPRIETOR.

yachtsmen. Hundreds availed themselves of their invitation. and enjoyed the lake breeze under the shade and also the bounteous feast that had been prepared. The yachtsmen were kept busy all day long taking the relays of young peple out upon the waves. Toward evening the last party went out further than usual. when a sudden gale sprang up from the "nor'west" causing the waves to roll dangerously high. As the little vessel approached the shore and when about 200 yards distant. a strong sea swept over her deck and swamped the little craft completely. For a moment it looked to those upon the shore that the entire party. crew and all. would be drowned. Men mounted horses and rushed into the angry surf. while others plunged in on foot. to the rescue. Luckily. the waves carried the unfortunates into shallow water and as some were good swimmers. with the help of the rescuers. no one was drowned.

In the year 1871 the municipal election chose the following city officers. to-wit: Mayor—Lyman S. Wood. Aldermen—Wm. Wordsworth. Solomon D. Chase. Councilors—Jacob Houtz. Abram Noe. Thos. L. Mendenhall. Recorder—F. C. Boyer. Marshal—Oscar Crandall. Treasurer—John Maycock. F. P. Whitmore was appointed January 22, 1872. vice Oscar Crandall. resigned.

On the 26th day of June, 1872. Nephi E. Hall was shot down at the corner of Johnson and Main streets. by Charles Bowlden. from the effects of which he died the day following. The trouble between the two young men and which led to the tragedy. began the evening of the 25th of that month, at a dance held at the Third Ward school house. and was caused by drink and jealousy. Some hot words and blows were exchanged. but friends intervened and the beligerents were prevented from making further disturbance by being escorted to their homes. The next day. as Nephi Hall with some of his friends

were sitting in front of Johnson's hall. Bowlden came down the street. mounted. When he arrived nearly opposite the crowd. Nephi arose and went out to meet him. when some hard words were passed when. as quick as a flash. Bowlden drew his pistol that was at his saddle bow and shot his assailant. who immediately turned and ran toward the Johnson home. leaping a 4-foot fence at a single bound and fell. He was carried into the Johnson residence where he died. Bowlden gave himself up to the officers. and a few days afterward he had a hearing before Mayor Sanford. He seemed to have a case of self defense and was given his liberty.

In 1872-3. the people were engaged in entering their lands at the land office at Salt Lake City: by pre-emption and homestead entry. Many began to move out to settle Mapleton. Previously that locality had been used mostly as a herd ground for milch cows and work cattle. It is claimed that Chas. Malmstrom built the first permanent residence upon the bench on the claim now owned by Stephen D. Johnson. During these years the Springville townsite was entered at the land office for a city. and most of the older deeds to the city lots were sign_d by Cyrus Sanford. as mayor. the residents having lived for over twenty years without legal titles to their homes.

The city officers elected in 1873 were as follows: L. S. Wood. mayor: Solomon D. Chase and J. W. Bissell. aldermen: Alexander Robertson. John Maycock and Hugh M. Dougall. councilors: F. C. Boyer, recorder: F. P. Whitmore. marshal. Richard Thorn. jr.. was appointed recorder March 27. 1875. vice Boyer. who was called on a mission. Abner Worthen was appointed marshal April 27. 1874.

In the winter of 1873–4 the United Order was the chief topic of discussion by pulpit and press. President Brigham Young declared that the time had

come to enter this Holy Order. The
people, however, were not united upon
this question and there was quite an
under-current of opposition. However, the teachers went to every family
and asked them to agree to put their
property into the order, which most of
them agreed to do "when the time
came." But the time never came and
but little was turned in, and the pro-
ject failed "for want of means to start
it with." Moreover, the people were
called together for the purpose of
organization, which was fully accomplished by selecting every officer necessary to conduct many kinds of business, from the general superintendent
down to the chief soap-maker. Nothing was left undone that voting could
accomplish, and then the people returned to their homes to pursue the
even tenor of their way. Under the
auspices of the order E. R. Brown
established a shoe shop and made most
excellent boots and shoes, but it soon
drifted into an individual concern.

George Mason also for a year conducted
what was called the United Order
Meat Market.

In 1876 the Co-op grist mill was constructed and the Co-op store on State
street built, in which a larger stock of
goods were displayed than ever before.
At this time, and previously, the Co-op
paid very large dividends—as high as
25 per cent, semi-annually. It was in
every sense "the peoples' store," as
there were more than four hundred
stockholders, who met semi-annually
to hear business reports from the directors. Many of the stockholders were
not in favor of paying such large dividends to the people, and instead putting
by a goodly per cent, as a sinking fund
to put the business on a safe and permanent basis. The majority, however,
voted down any proposition to curtail
the dividend payments. Thus it ran
along for a few years without opposition and with no increase of the capital
stock, until a time when the predicted
opposition came from other merchants

FARMING IMPLEMENT HOUSE OF JOHN R. KINDRED.

and the Co-op stock began to decline. The dividends commenced to decrease until none were paid and the value of the stock declined to forty cents on the dollar, when it was purchased by the G. S. Wood Mercantile Company and became a private concern.

In 1875 Lyman S. Wood was elected to succeed himself as mayor of the city. The aldermen were J. W. Bissell and John S. Boyer. Councilors—Wm. D. Johnson, Oliver B. Huntington, Wm. Bringhurst. Recorder—R. H. Thorn. Marshal — Ira Sanford. Richard L. Mendenhall was appointed marshal Dec. 4, 1875. F. C. Boyer was appointed recorder June 26, 1876. Myron E. Crandall was appointed marshal March 7, 1877.

In the year 1875 the Mutual Improvement Associations were organized here under the general order from the Presidency of the Latter-Day Saints church. Foremost among the members in that day were Wm. M. Bromley, John S. Boyer, James E. Hall, Aaron Johnson, F. C. Boyer, L. D. Crandall, D. C. Johnson and Abram Noe. Much interest was manifested, quite a library was gathered and a membership paper entitled "The Endeavor" was published, D. C. Johnson being the principal editor. Of the Young Ladies', Mrs. Lydia Johnson was president and Eliza Haymond vice-president, Mrs. Mary Whiting, Caroline Whiting and Colista Perry were among the prominent officers. These associations have continued until the present time and have had a numerous membership. They are now divided into ward associations.

In the spring of 1876 Aaron Johnson, Sylvester Perry and Jesse Ballinger were called to colonize some point upon the Colorado river in Arizona. They fitted themselves out and left early in February, making the journey in safety. A colony was formed at the Sunset crossing. A permanent settlement was laid out, crops put in and some houses built, when a great flood came and

HON. WILLIAM M. ROYLANCE

washed everything away. After remaining a year or two they were released to come home. Ballinger, Perry and Johnson returned, but Whiting remained and subsequently moved to Mexico.

This spring the farms in Hobble Creek canyon were re-located. Most of the claims had been taken up as early as 1857-8, but owing to the Indian difficulties they had been abandoned. From 1856 to 1876 almost continuously the canyon had been used as a public summer range, where dry stock was herded from April until the "Big field" was opened in October when the cattle were "rounded up," driven out and wintered in the big west field, which was then fenced in common and made a fine winter range. The herdsmen in the canyon received as compensation so much per head for the summer care of the stock.

The people chose for their municipal officers in 1877 the mayor of the previous two years: J. W. Bissell and John S. Boyer as aldermen: Wm. Bringhurst, Wm. D. Johnson and Abram Noe as councilors; F. C. Boyer for recorder, M. E. Crandall for marshal and J. W. Bissell for treasurer. Henry Bartlett was appointed marshal June 5, 1878. Wm. Clyde was also appointed marshal Dec. 4, 1878, and Uel Stewart on April 25, 1879.

In 1877 Milan Packard projected and commenced to build the Utah & Pleasant Valley Railroad. Early in the spring the surveyors, Smith & Dorenus, had located the line, which was commenced at the Utah Central yards down Center street. This Utah Central Railroad, so named at first, started at Ogden and had been completed through Utah county in the autumn of 1873. From this depot, one and one-fourth miles from town, the Utah & Pleasant Valley started, running thence east to the corner of the Square, thence turning south and running in the middle of State street out in the direction of the Big Hollow, and thence to Spanish Fork canyon. Early in the spring men and teams were at work upon the grade. The oracles said it would never be completed, but Mr. Packard kept on and the work steadily progressed. On the 27th of April while the camps were at work at the mouth of Spanish Fork canyon a big snow storm set in and kept falling until twenty-five inches had fallen on the level. The grading progressed up to Thistle this year and toward autumn contracts for

ties were let for the "Calico road," as it was facetiously called for the reason that Mr. Packard paid principally out of his store, which he had started the previous year and was the first one to come in conflict with the Co-op store.

On the 10th day of May, 1877, Bishop Aaron Johnson died at the age of 72 years. At his funeral all business was suspended, for the entire people felt that they had lost a father. He had been the bishop of the ward for twenty years and had been at the head of all the public affairs during those years. He was known as a philanthrophist far and wide for his benevolent acts. At the time of his decease more than $10,000 was due him from the people of Utah for supplies of various kinds that he had advanced during the two decades of his administration. The value of the public works performed during his Bishopric is given as $132,000, exclusive of tithing.

In the early summer of 1878 the track of the narrow guage railroad was laid up to State street and the first train of flat cars came up to the corner of the Square. The people turned out en masse

RESIDENCE OF BISHOP NEPHI PACKARD

STORE BUILDING OF H. T. REYNOLDS & CO.

to celebrate the event, and the brass band was out to make music for the occasion. The good-natured crowd literally took possession of the train, and Conductor George Goss, seeing no alternative but to submit, gave orders to the effect that all should be carried from the terminus to the depot and return. The flats were packed with a swarming mass of humanity. The band was seated in front and the happy throng rode up and down many times during the afternoon and enjoyed the ride most intensely.

The voters of the city still continued the former mayor in office for 1879–80, and chose as aldermen John S. Boyer and Abram Noe. Wm. Bringhurst, Leonard J. Whitney and Wm. H. Kelsey held the councilors' seats. F. C. Boyer continued to record the minutes. F. P. Whitmore as marshal looked after the disorderly element. J. W. Bissell was treasurer, and Don C. Johnson assessed and collected the city taxes. It is to the credit of this administration that the City Hall was built and the pres-

ent trees in the park were planted.

In 1876 Mr. Packard pressed his road hard as far up as Mill Fork, with the track to Thistle, expending in the work over $60,000. At this time he tried to get the Utah county people to take hold and assist in constructing the road and own it and the coal fields. He also endeavored to get President John Taylor of the L. D. S. church to assist. President Taylor and John Sharp came down to Provo and with Bishop Bringhurst of Springville and other capitalists here entered into some negotiations which, however, were never consumated. Mr. Packard, after vainly endeavoring to get home capital to come to the rescue and help him through with the project, sold out to George Goss and others, and the goose that has been laying golden eggs for its owners ever since passed out of the hands of local people. So much in earnest was Mr. Packard that home people should own this road and coal fields that he went to President Taylor's office thirty minutes before he signed the papers transfering the property to other hands. Mr. Taylor informed him that he could not take hold of the matter. Thus it ended and the people of our town pursued the even tenor of their way. Large numbers engaged in freighting and railroading and many in timbering. The Johnson & Hall company shipped the first load of freight over the Utah & Pleasant Valley Ry., the same being ten carloads of ties for the Utah Central R'y and were loaded at Mill Fork.

Frank Straw, son of Mr. and Mrs. James Straw, was killed by a falling tree while engaged in getting out ties for this railroad.

The year 1880 marked a new era in educational matters in Springville. Prof. S. S. Hamill of Chicago gave a series of lessons in the art of elocution and many of our young people availed themselves of the opportunity. From that date a marked improvement has been observed in public speaking, reading and declamation.

In 1880, Geo. Leonard came to Springville and established a mission school, under the supervision of the Presbyterian Board. Miss Annie Noble was the first teacher. Mr. Leonard afterward built what is now known as the "Dinwoodey" school for a chapel in which Miss Mattie Vores, Miss Eugenia Munger and Miss Ray taught school. Mr. Leonard was the pastor of the Presbyterian congregation for some eight years and until the time of his death. He was a stirring, enterprising man and much beloved by his congregation, and was esteemed by all as an earnest, energetic upright man.

When the time for the municipal election came, in the autumn of 1881, L. S. Wood was again chosen as chief executive: Abram Noe and P. H. Boyer were elected aldermen: Wm. Bringhurst, W. H. Kelsey and John S. Boyer, were chosen as councilors: F. C. Boyer, recorder, F. P. Whitmore, marshal: J. W. Bissell, treasurer: D. C.

Johnson, assessor and collector. Nephi Packard and James Whitehead were appointed councilors, vice Bringhurst and Kelsey, resigned.

In 1882 a new company purchased the Utah & Pleasant Valley railroad, which was merged into the Rio Grande Western system.

This season much work was done by our people on the railroad, in lumbering and in furnishing timber. H. T. Reynolds & Co. then commenced their merchandising career. They purchased a small stock of goods from Geo. Manwaring and Samuel Alsworth. Their business was a success from the start and has grown under their skilful management to its present creditable proportions. D. C. Johnson, Bros. & James E. Hall, built a theater this year: the best, at that time, outside of Salt Lake City, in Utah Territory. It cost $10,000 and would seat 500 people. The stage was large enough, to put on any kind of a play, and was the scene of many performances by first-class companies. The scenery cost $1000 and was painted by Henry C. Tryon, of Chicago. A local troupe, members of S. S. Hamil's elocution class, became almost as good as professionals, being great favorites at home and through the southern part of the state. The more noted members of the Home Dramatic troupe were: J. M. Westwood, Aaron and Moses Johnson, C. W. Houtz, Mrs. Lydia M. Johnson, Luella Matson and Eliza Johnson. Later, Miss Viola Cook, Lulu and Lily Boyer, were added. In 1890 the beautiful opera house was burned to the ground, much to the sorrow of the general public.

In 1885, a planing mill was erected, at a cost of $5000 by Messrs. H. M. Dougall, D. C. Johnson, Fred Carter and E. J. Hall, which did a vast amount of labor for the carpenters and mechanics. It was reduced to ashes by the same fire that consumed the theater.

On the 17th day of February, 1883,

Bishop William Bringhurst died, after a lingering illness of some weeks duration. He was born in Pennsylvania, November 18th, 1818: was married to Ann Dilworth, March 25th, 1845: joined the L. D. S. church the same year and one year after moved to Nauvoo, Illinois. which place he left in the year 1846 and wintered at Winter Quarters in 1847: coming to Utah October 10th of the same year. He lived in Salt Lake City and Big Cottonwood until 1852, when he was called to go to Parowan, to assist in building up that settlement. In 1855, he was called on a mission to Las Vegas, California, remaining there some years until released to return north. In the year 1860, he came to Springville to live, where he was afterward identified as a leading and enterprising citizen. He was a successful merchant and business man and held many civil positions in the municipality.

On the 4th day of March, 1883, Nephi Packard was set apart as Bishop of the Ward, vice Wm. Bringhurst, deceased. His counselors were: James Whitehead and Benjamin T. Banchard. Nothing worthy of special note occurred during this year. The people were engaged in their usual pursuits. Our city had grown to about 2,500 people: business had increased exceedingly all along the line.

At the August election, Mayor L. S. Wood still was declared elected for another two years. Abram Noe and Lucien D. Crandall gave bonds as aldermen. Nephi Packard, Uel Stewert and Alexander Robertson qualified as councilors. J. W. Bissell held the key to the treasury. Oscar Mower wore the marshal's star. Myron E. Crandall assessed and collected the taxes.

CHAPTER XVIII.

THE year 1884-5, developed nothing out of the usual routine of affairs in our city, in a progressive or business way, but many of our citizens were very much discommoded in their avocations in life by the continuous and rigid enforcement of the Edmunds Law, for the offense of polygamy and unlawful co-habitation. During these years a great number of persons, and indeed, up into 1890, were compelled to take to the "Underground," or go to prison, and quite a number chose the latter.

In 1885, occurred the regular biennial election of city officials, which resulted in the selection of the following persons: Lyman S. Wood, to succeed himself, as chief executive. Aldermen—Abram Noe, R. A. Deal. Councilors—Nephi Packard, L. D. Crandall, Alexander Robertson. Recorder—James Caffrey. Marshal—James E. Hall. Treasurer—Joseph W. Bissell. Assessor and collector—D. C. Johnson. Oscar M. Mower was appointed councilor, May 5th, 1886, vice L. D. Crandall, resigned.

In 1886-7, the tide of events passed along, with seed time and harvest: improving and enlarging the farming area: freighting and railroad building.

In 1886, the Hungerford academy was built for academic purposes, under the management of J. A. L. Smith, who was also the first principal and under whose tutorship the institution grew to be one of the foremost educational institutes in our county, at which many of our young men graduated, under the tutelage of Prof. Smith, I. N. Smith, Willis Marshal and Miss Ora Gates, and a competent corps of teachers.

THE HARRISON HOTEL, PROFESSOR GEORGE HARRISON, PROPRIETOR.

At the autumn election of 1887, the electors of the city selected L. S. Wood, for the tenth time, as mayor; retaining R. A. Deal and Abram Noe, as aldermen; electing Alexander Robertson, John S. Boyer and John Tuckett, as councilors; James Caffrey, for recorder; James E. Hall, as Marshal and James Whitehead as treasurer.

In 1888, Deal Bros. & Mendenhall, having saved $1000 each, of ready money, concluded to go into the mercantile business and built their present store, where they have since done a large amount of the business of the town and where they continue at the old stand. They also have an extensive railroad grading outfit.

In the fall of 1889, the bi-ennial election resulted in selecting Alex Robertson, for mayor; Abram Noe and J. W. Bissell as alderman, and for councilmen, John Tuckett, Henry T. Reynolds and R. A. Deal; for recorder, James Caffrey; marshal, James E. Hall, and John H. Bringhurst, as treasurer.

During the years 1889-90, under the marshalship of James E. Hall, the prohibition ordinance, which had become a law, began to be enforced with some rigor and in a way to terrify law-breakers and to meet the hearty approval of a large majority of the people.

In the late autumn of 1889, the theater hall, that had been the pride and admiration of the people for eight years, took fire about 3 o'clock in the morning and in connection with the planing mill, where the fire fiend started, was reduced to ashes. The fire consumed $20,000 worth of property. Those who lost most were: Milan Packard, H. M. Dougall, Don and Moses Johnson and E. J. Hall.

In the year 1890, the Woman's Suffrage association, of Springville, was organized with Mrs. S. A. Boyer, as president; M. V. N. Hall and Mary Jane Matson, as vice-presidents. The society grew in magnitude and became a political factor in the subsequent years, as the territory approached the threshold of statehood. In 1896, Mrs. S. A. Boyer was selected to go to Washington, D. C.. as one of the two delegates. from this state. to the national convention of Woman Suffragists.

In the spring of 1891. the people of the Territory of Utah divided on party lines and Springville followed in line. On the evening of the 30th of May there was a public meeting called. for the purpose of organizing a Republican club, at which D. C. Johnson. John Henry Smith and John M. Zane. were the speakers. After the meeting a roll was prepared and there were one dozen signers within the next few days. The week following the Democrats called a meeting at the City hall. that was numerously attended. at which the principles of the Democratic party were set forth by Judges J. M. Judd. John B. Milner and Wilson M. Dusenberry. which resulted in an organization. after the session of over sixty members.

In May. 1891. President Harrison and party passed through our city and made a stay of fifteen minutes. when he made a short speech and greeted with a hearty handshake. the G. A. R. veterans. that stood in a body to receive him. He praised our valley and the indomitable energy displayed by the early settlers in wresting it from barbarism. . John Wanamaker. postmaster general. made some pleasant and appropriate remarks. to the assembled thousands. who made the welkin ring with their hearty cheers as the palace on wheels rolled away.

In June the "Old Folks" of the territory came to Springville for their annual excursion and were entertained by our people most royally at Bishop Packard's grove. It was voted as one of the most successful social affairs ever engaged in by the Springville people.

On the 20th day of August. 1891. the first newspaper was started in the city. under the title of the "Springville Independent." with, Newman H. Mix. as editor and Geo. F. Saunders. as publisher. On March 25th. 1892. D. C. Johnson took the editorial tripod. with Geo. F. Saunders as manager. Wayne Johnson and D. C. Johnson. jr. as typos. In January 1893. Saunders sold out and Johnson conducted the sheet until May 10th. 1895. when he disposed of his interests to D. P. Felt. who managed the weekly until August 18th. 1897. W. F. Gibson leased the sheet until June 1st. 1898. at which time Samuel M. Leroy took the helm until November 1st. 1898. when W. F. Gibson again assumed the editorial department. with Elliot N. Jordan as manager. which position he still occupies.

In 1891. the Springville Banking company was organized and commenced business in the Caffrey building. but moved to their new. and present quarters in the autumn of 1892. The chief projectors of the bank were: Milan Packard. E. A. Deal. H. T. Reynolds. F. C. Boyer. James Caffrey was the first cashier. who was succeeded by H. L. Cummings. who now occupies the position.

In August. this year. the first election on national party lines was held.

CYRUS E. DALLIN

DR. C. J. PETERSON'S DRUG STORE.

The Republicans selected D. C. Johnson as the head of the ticket and R. A. Deal became the leader of the Democratic element. After a good-natured campaign, that was full of vim and enthusiasm, the Democratic nominees were elected by about 100 majority and were as follows: Mayor—R. A. Deal. Councilors—L S Wood, T. L. Mendenhall, R. H. Thorn, Alexander Robertson, Albert Harner, Wm. M. Roylance, Henry T. Reynolds. Recorder—James Caffrey. Marshal — James E. Hall. Treasurer—Joseph S. Storrs. Assessor and collector—James Straw. Justice of the Peace—Joseph W. Bissell. Edwin Lee was appointed water-master and D. C. Johnson city attorney with Dr. C. J. Peterson as quarantine physician.

In 1892, a wave of building enthusiasm struck the town, and as a result: the majestic store building of H. T. Reynolds & Co.; the model bank build-

ing and the Bonney and Miner blocks, graced the main street. while a large number of private dwelings were constructed in various parts of the city.

This year the people purchased the Rio Grande Western's right of way, on State street, and its track was moved to Fourth street, where commodious freight and passenger depots have been erected.

This year, the climax was reached in regard to the suppression of the liquor trafic in our city. The policy was "no compromise," and the ordinance was fearlessly enforced by the marshal, city attorney and justice of the peace. Several persons were apprehended on a charge of selling liquor without license and in violation of the city ordinances, "in such cases made and provided," were dealt with severely, which resulted in the financial ruin of those who presisted in vending the intoxicants.

On the 15th day of April, of this year, our city, which had been divided into ecclesiastical wards, were given bishops to preside over them, as follows: First Ward—John Tuckett, with Chas. Berry and Van O. Fullmer, to act as counselors. Second Ward—Loren H. Harmer; Seymour B. Snow and Simon E. Dalton, for counselors. Third Ward—Geo. R. Hill; Lucien D. Crandall and Oscar M. Mower, as counsellors. Fourth Ward—Joseph S. Loynd; James E. Hall. Marion M. Johnson as counselors.

On the 22th of June the Johnsons held a re-union to commemorate the 88th birthday of Aaron Johnson. All the first who had come to Springville to make their homes, were invited, in addition to the members of the family, there being over 320 persons present. That day the Johnsons, with their friends, held the City hall and grounds and with program of music, speeches and songs, feasting and dancing, a profitable and pleasant day was spent. For years previously the idea of celebrating by famlily re-unions had been growing and put into practice and since then have continued among the leading famlies in our city, notably: Deals, Crandalls, Sanfords, Clarks, Mendenhalls and others, and the good old custom seems to have become a regular yearly observance.

In the autumn of 1893, the Democratic voters of the city, after a warm contest, succeeded in electing their ticket which called for the retention of Mayor R. A. Deal. Conncilors, John S. Boyer, Joseph S. Loynd, James Caffrey, Joseph Harner and Alexander Robertson. Recorder, R. H. Thorn. Treasurer, Joseph H. Storrs. Justice of the Peace, Abram Noe. The appointed officers were: Fred Dunn, city physician; Edwin Lee, water-master; D. C. Johnson, city attorney.

On the afternoon of the Fourth of July, 1893, a few veterans of the Black Hawk war, met upon the public square

and were talking over the old troublous war times and it was there agreed to have a re-union of the Black Hawk warriors, their families and friends, sometime during the ensuing winter. The prime movers in the affair were: George Harrison, Edwin Lee, Joseph M. Westwood, Albert Harmer, Francis Beardall and Walter Wheeler. On January 1st, 1894, there was a meeting at which, in addition to the above named, were present: Thomas A. Brown, Elial Curtis and Samuel Bulkley, and it was there arranged to invite all the comrades of the Black Hawk war residing in the county to meet at Reynold's hall, January 24, 1894, for a grand ball and picnic. There was a local society organized about the same time called the "Springville Comrades of the Black Hawk War." The first captain was J. M. Westwood; adjutant and quartermaster, Thomas A. Brown. The present captain is Edwin Lee; adjutant, J. M. Westwood; quarter-master, Albert Harmer. From this association evolved the present state organization,

DR. GEO. L. SMART.

known as the "Utah Indian War Veteran's Association," under whose auspices the great encampment was held this year (1900) and whose officers are: Joseph M. Westwood, commander-in-chief; Thomas A. Brown, adjutant and quarter-master. During the past year the "Home Guards" and "Walker and Tintic War Veterans" have held receptions, balls and feasts, which have been patronized and looked forward to as events to be prized for their social and enlivening character.

On the 25th day of January, 1894, the Black Hawk War Veterans held their first re-union, at Reynold's hall, commencing at 2 o'clock, p. m., and continuing, with an interval for supper, until 4 o'clock, a. m., next day. There were 111 veterans present, from various parts of the county. On the arrival of the visiting delegations at Springville they were met with sleighs, under the direction of George Harrison, and taken to the homes of the Springville comrades, where old acquaintances were revived and stories of the war times recounted. At 2 o'clock, p. m., order was called by Captain F. P. Whitmore, and the Springville comrades opened with a song, entitled "The Black Hawk War." F. C. Boyer made an eloquent speech of

welcome. At 6 o'clock, p. m., the supper hour arrived. A tent was pitched outside and a fire kept burning, reminding all of the early camping days. At intervals between dances, speeches were made by Orson Creer, of Spanish Fork, an original poem was recited by Milando Pratt, and Albert Jones sang an old-time song, composed during the Sanpete campaign of 1866-7. Levi N. Kendall, a Utah pioneer, made remarks, and Colonel Page, of Payson, recounted some incidents of the war. Benjamin Driggs told about compaigning in Sanpete; D. C. Johnson told of the fight upon the Diamond and the gallant ride of Noakes, Curtis and Stewart; John Tanner, of Payson, told how he got out of a certain scrape at Nephi; B. W. Brown narrated his experiences at the fight at the Gravelly ford. Thus, with music and song the first happy re-union of the Indian fighters of Utah, passed into history.

Since then these re-unions have been held annually, also a mid-winter dance and festival. Their last grand encampment was held at the Provo Lake resort, on the 8th, 9th and 10th, of August, 1900, at which those who were present greatly enjoyed the exercises.

CHAPTER XIX.

IN the year of 1895, sericulture was for the second time introduced into the city, and practically proven that it was an industry that can be made of great use and benefit, though it is still in its infancy. The promoters of this scheme were: Mesdames Kate Dougall, Zebina Alleman, John Conover, Elizabeth Packard, M. V. N. Hall and Celestie Whitmore. A very superior article of silk has been raised and put into fabric, of a very superior

quality. It is believed by some of those ladies, that our city will yet be the seat of a great silk industry.

On the 20th day of November, of this year, the Mutual Improvement Association held a four day's fair in Reynold's hall, that had a first-class display of articles usually exhibited at county fairs and was visited by thousands of our citizens, who heartily praised the exhibits. The evenings were enlivened by music, songs and speeches. The affair was a brilliant success. from every point of view. What a contrast to the fair held in the old unplastered school house of forty years ago!

In the the autumn of 1895, the municipal election was very warmly contested. The Democrats nominated R. A. Deal and the Republicans. Samuel M. Davis. The Republicans with the Springville vote elected the entire ticket. but the Mapletonians. who had not voted the municipal ticket for several years previously. voted here, and elected the entire Democratic ticket. with the exception of Joseph M. Westwood. Republican nominee for city justice. For the state ticket the Republicans had a majority of six. The votes. for the head of the ticket. were as follows: Springville—Deal. 311: Davis. 324. Mapleton—Deal. 27: Davis. 11. Wm. M. Roylance. was elected to the lower House of the State Legislature.

The following officers were inaugurated January 1st.. 1896:

Mayor—R. A. Deal. Councilors—Henry T. Reynolds. James E. Hall. J. S. Loynd, Alexander Robertson, J. S. Scott. Recorder—A. J. Southwick. Marshal—George A. Storrs, (Silas E. Clark was appointed on December 7th. 1897, vice George A. Storrs. resigned): Treasurer—Joseph H. Storrs. Justice —J. M. Westwood. Water-master— Walter Bird, (Edwin Lee was appointed February. 1897): City Attorney— Samuel R. Thurman.

On Monday evening. February 8th. 1897. a Tent of the Knights of the Maccabees was organized in Springville. a protective and fraternal organization. under the supervision of Deputy Supreme Commander J. W. Wright. of Salt Lake City. with the following officers: Sir Knights—Frederick Dunn. past commander: C. E. Christensen, commander: Andrew Berkley. lieutenant commander: Frank Haymond. record keeper: Thomas R. Kelly. finance

keeper: E. J. Stanson. chaplain: J. M. Whitmore. sergeant: J. R. Meneray, master-at-arms; F. J. Maack. 1st master of guards: John Marten. 2nd master of guards: Dr. F. Dunn. physician: I. N. Whittaker. sentinel: Wm. Brown. picket.

In the last three years the membership in Springville has increased to over 100 and the order now numbers 103 members in good standing. Within the last year they have organized a very fine band. which takes no second rank in our county for all-around excellence.

In the autumn of 1897. two municipal tickets were in the political field—Democratic and Non-partisan. James E. Hall ran for mayor on the Democratic ticket and Nephi Packard on that of the Non-partisan. The election was a tame affair. only about 70 per cent. of the entire vote being polled. The officers elected were: James E. Hall. Mayor: P. E. Houtz. recorder: Luella Haymond. treasurer: Silas E. Clark. marshal: R. H. Thorn. city justice: O.

DR. FRED DUNN.

LIEUTENANT W. B. DOUGALL.

B. Huntington jr. Loren Harmer, H. T. Reynolds, J. H. Storrs and J. S. Loynd, councilors.

On the 17th of November, 1897, occurred one of the most deplorable accidents in the city's history—that of the shooting of Marshal Silas E. Clark, at the City hall. On the evening aforesaid, James Whitmore and Joseph Whitehead, met at the marshal's office, to arrange for the capture of certain tramps, who were infesting and pillaging the neighborhood and were loading their pistols preparatory to going out, when Whitmore in returning his pistol to its scabbard, in some unaccountable manner discharged it. It was a 32-calibre revolver and the ball struck the marshal in the abdomen, inflicting a fatal wound. The best medical skill available was secured, but without avail. He died five days after he received the wound. S. E. Clark was born January 20th, 1854, in Iowa, and came to Utah with his parents in 1861.

The year 1898 was a year filled with military display and war alarms,

and the patriotic feeling of our townfolk was wrought up to the highest pitch of enthusiasm and were kept at a high tension during the entire year, and the succeeding one. On the 11th day of April, Colonel F. Grant, of the Utah National Guard, Salt Lake City, and Lieutenant-Colonel Denhalter, of Provo, came down to Springville for the purpose of organizing a militia company. A rousing meeting was held in the City hall, and stirring speeches were made by D. C. Johnson, Colonels Grant and Denhalter, showing the necessity of preparing for war in the time of peace. After the meeting, the following persons volunteered to form a company: Wallace Hope, Wm. Gibson, J. Johnson, Nephi Whitehead, P. E. Houtz, E. J. Stanson, Elliott N. Jordan, C. E. Swenson, T. M. Haymond, jr; Aner Humphrey, C. F. Parry, Stanley Staten, Ross M. Bonny Joseph Smith, Clint Bryan, C. J. Roylance, Jessie Strang, Milan L. Crandall, Moses Dougall and L. Whitehead. For a few days the canvass was continued, but no other names were added, and the organization of a company was not completed. April 20th was a day long to be remembered by young and old, especially by the young, who had never seen an army of men going to actual war. When it became known that the 24th Regiment, (colored) from Fort Douglas, had marching orders for Cuba and that they would be along about 11 o'clock, a. m., the entire population turned out to greet them; our 600 pupils of the public schools being present under Superintendent Rydalch. Nearly every school child held a small flag. As section 1 of the train bearing the troops came into the yards, "America" greeted them, from the multitude. As soon as the train slacked up, hundreds of black faces protruded from the windows and the platforms were packed with the dusky soldiers, whose black faces lighted up with joy and whose honest hearts beat in unison

with the singing throng. When
the train pulled out, each warrior's
hand bore a small flag given him by
the school children, which were waved
heartily as they rounded the curve.
followed by the cheers of the now
thoroughly enthused crowd. Section 2
received a similar greeting and the colored troops assured the citizens that
they would give a good account of
themselves. and "Remember the
Maine."

On the 28th of April. Captain R. W.
Young came down on the train for the
purpose of enlisting men for the Spanish-American war. He was met by D.
C. Johnson and others. and after a few
introductions. H. L. Cummings offered
the office of the bank as a recruiting
office. which was accepted. D. C.
Johnson procured a flag from C. E.
Tranchell and displayed it from the
upper window and then announced the
United States recruiting office open and
ready for enlistments. There were no
speeches made. to awaken the enthusiasm of the assembled crowd. it being
thought best to allow every man to
use his own cool judgment to decide
whether he desired to serve his country
as a soldier or not. The terms of enlistment were. "for two years or during the war." and the ages

SAMUEL DALLIN.

were to be between 18 and 45: height.
5 feet 4 inches to 6 feet: weight. 135 to
165 pounds. Samuel Dallin was the
first to enlist and passed a successful
examination before Dr. F. Dunn. and
during the day the following boys enlisted in the order named: E. N. Jordan.
N. S. Nelson. Ezra Oakley. Wm. Tipton.
George Houtz. Antony Ethier. Frank

Harmer. Stanley Staten. Aner
Humphrey, Evans Chase. Luther
Stewart and Fred Dart. of Spanish
Fork. gave in their names here.
G. W. Page. Wm. B. Louder.
Moroni Tervoirt. from Payson.
In the evening Captain Young
went to Mt. Pleasant to open a
recruiting station there. and left
word that D. C. Johnson would
open the office on Saturday.
April 30th. for further enlist-
ments, when the following names
were added: Canute Swenson.
J. Wilk Streeper. Wm. H. Liter.
John C. Bell. Harry Hanford. a
Springville boy. enlisted at

J. W. STREEPER.

D. C. FULLMER.

STANLEY STATEN.

ANER HUMPHREY.

Eureka. Later, Wm. B. Dougall enlisted in the Engineer Corps. A number of the recruits did not fill the physical requirements, and a number who did, were not mustered into the service; for the reason that the state enlisted double the number apportioned in the call. On the day after the last enlistment, a self appointed committee consisting of Hon. Wm. Roylance, ex-Mayor Deal, J. M. Westwood and D. C. Johnson, arranged for a reception to the volunteers at the City hall. The appointed hour found the hall crowded, with the band and

Mandolin club present. Old Glory occupied a central position. D. C. Johnson called order and named Hon. Wm. M. Roylance as chairman, who made an address. "God Save Our Nation," was rendered by Miss Katherine Dougall. Thomas R. Kelly, Myron E. Crandall and F. N. West. Mayor James E. Hall followed with a speech. The band and Mandolin club rendered patriotic music. The vast audience

DON C. JOHNSON, JR.

was enthused with speeches by Thomas Dallin. C. D. Evans and F. C. Boyer. "Go Where Glory Awaits Thee" was then rendered by the Glee club: speeches were delivered by John S. Boyer. G. E. Anderson. D. C. Johnson and Prof. W. E. Rydalch. Miss Myrtle Hall recited "The American Flag". The volunteers occupied a conspicuous position upon the stage and each responded to a hearty call by a brief speech.

WM. TIPTON.

teeming with patriotic sentiment. Stanley Staten said: "If Old Glory ever goes down in defeat, seventeen American gentlemen from Springville will go down with it." which sally was received with roars of satisfaction. Just as the chairman was taking his place, he was handed, and read, a telegram from Don C. Johnson, jr., announcing that he had enlisted at Salt Lake City, but could not get down to the reception.

On May 1st, when the morning papers brought the news of

FRANK HARMER.

Dewey's glorious victory at Manila, the town went wild. Everything in the town. that could be made to shoot, was touched off and flags streamed and fluttered from every public building and many private residences.

On May 5th, our volunteers went, by the morning train, to Salt Lake City. to be mustered into the service of the United States and a thousand people cheered them as they departed. while mothers. with many a thrill of pain. felt an impending sense of danger hovering over their loved ones and prayed for their safe return.

Aner Humphrey. Stanley Staten. Wm. Tipton and Frank Harmer. served in the Philippine campaign in Battery A., Utah Light Artillery and Don C. Johnson. in Battery B. All performed gallant service and returned to their homes alive and well. Wilk Streeper and Will Liter. went to Jacksonville Fla.. with Torrey's Rough Riders. and Samuel Dallin. served under Captain Caine. in California.

On Saturday. June 28th. a bold bank robbery was perpetrated at the Springville bank. Two rough looking men drove into town about 10 o'clock. a. m.. from Mapleton. in a buggy with a single horse attached. and hitched in front of the bank and walked into the building. Cashier. H. L. Cummings. had just gone out to answer a telephone call and Assistant Cashier A. O. Packard was alone. The fellows made inquiry as to whether any money had been left on deposit for them and on being answered in the negative. expressed surprise. and engaged Packard in conversation for a moment. in relation to the matter. At length Mr. Packard turned from the teller's window. and as he again turned his head toward it. found that he was looking down the barrels of two formidable revolvers and was commanded in a stern voice. "Throw up your hands!" The hands referred to immediately took the attitude of prayer and while the suppris-

ed cashier was kept in this position. the disengaged robber went quickly behind the desk and swept all the money in sight into his coat pocket—$3.000 in all. While the hands of the cashier were unable to serve him, he managed. unperceived, to touch the electric alarm with his foot. which had connections with Deal Bros. & Mendenhall's and H. T. Reynolds & Co's. stores, where the clerks were instantly on the alert. In the meantime the desperadoes rushed quickly out. leaped into their buggy and lashed their horse to the top of its speed in the direction of Mapleton. Clarence L. Crandall, Henry T. Reynolds. Joseph H. Storrs and Marshal Gemmell. within ten minutes. were mounted and on the trail of the absconding thieves. while several citizens. well armed. jumped into the wagon of Thomas Kerswell. that was just at hand, and was lashing after the first party. Just on the raise of Mapleton bench the robbers met Thomas Snelson. who was in a cart coming to town. and as their horse was nearly winded. they demanded Snelson's horse. and enforced their request at the point of a pistol. Snelson did not deem it advisable to demur and got down in less than no time. when one of the outlaws leaped onto the horse's back and the other threw Snelson $46.50 in silver as they again urged their steeds forward at their utmost speed. As they neared the mouth of Hobble creek canyon the pursuers were within shooting distance and commenced to send a few shots ahead. which compelled the freebooters to leave their animals and take to the cover of the dense thicket. just where the little dugway turns to enter the canyon's mouth. and were all out of sight in a moment. and all was still save the murmur of the creek. and the sighing of the answering trees. While the advance parties took strategic positions to prevent the escape of the bold robbers. other parties rapidly arrived from town and in one hour fifty

BARBER SHOP OF AMOS A. BROWN.

persons arrived on wheels, horses and vehicles of every description. At the point where the malefactors left the road, $18.50 was found in the dust. Guards were put around the thicket, (about forty acres in area) and preparation made to drag the mazy thicket for the bandits. While the guards were being stationed George Packard, Wm. Clyde, Jas. B. Whitehead and James Whitmore discovered the chief bank robber carefully concealed under the dense thicket and induced him to come out into the open, at the point of several shot guns. He was thoroughly soaked with water, having waded the creek and he had about $2,000 of the treasure with him.

He had no arms, as he had concealed them, probably seeing that defiance would be futile against such odds. Sheriff Geo. A. Storrs, who had just arrived from Provo, in answer to a telegram, took charge of the prisoner and sent him to town, in irons. Preparations for a thorough search after the remaining robber were made, under the direction of Deputy Sheriff Brown, of Provo, and Marshal Gemmell. The thicket was to be entered at a point where the deserted buggy still stood. One party under the direction of Deputy Brown, consisting of Joseph Allen, Wm Kearns, Daniel Crandall, Joseph Wing and Stephen D. Johnson entered the brush at intervals of from six to eight feet. D. C. Johnson, David A. Crandall, John Clark and others, advanced at a point four rods further north, while some thirty others were advantageously disposed on the bluff, just in the rear. Within one minute some one in Brown's party called out, "Keep your places all! Here he is!" Everybody was at once on the alert. Some words of parley were exchanged with the desperado, and then five or six shots were fired, quickly, and the cry rang out: "My God! I'm shot! There was a swirling of the willows as positions were changed and then all was quiet for a moment, then a voice said: "Keep steady, we'll get him!" A few more shots were fired in quick succession and then a voice said: "There!

You'll never rob another bank!" At the scene of combat Joseph Allan was seen sitting on the bank of the canal, with his leg broken by a ball from the bandit's pistol, having pluckily returned shot for shot. He was tenderly carried out and placed in a vehicle, for transit home, while the dead freebooter was dragged from his lair, by Sheriff Storrs, and placed in a wagon, when all returned to town. Joseph Allan subsequently had his leg amputated and received $350 of the $500 reward for the capture of Maxwell, the robber who was captured alive, and $1,000 from the state. The bank paid for his doctor's services, and lost about $600 which was never recovered.

CHAPTER XX.

IN 1899, George Maycock was appointed as Bishop of the First Ward, vice John Tuckett, resigned, with John Manwaring and Willis Strong as counsellors. On the 19th day of August, the hearts of our people were made glad by the return of the Springville members of the Utah Batteries to their homes, when the entire population turned out and gave them a royal welcome. With cheers, music and flag displays, they were escorted to the City hall, where a great feast had been prepared. Here fathers, mothers, sisters, brothers and friends, made the glad hours speed most delightfully for the brave cannoneers. The other volunteers had returned previously, and were received with glad shouts of joy. Don C. Fullmer, jr., who returned late in the autumn; having served in the Philippines with the Nevada cavalry, was also given a royal reception.

Melvin Harmer, who enlisted on the 21st day of August, 1899, in C Troop,

11th Cavalry, for service in the Philippines, returned home on the 17th day

MAYOR MONT JOHNSON

of September, 1900, and his n u m e r o u s friends greeted him on the s e m i-centennial day, at home.

This autumn the Lehi S u g a r company built a branch factory at this place, for slicing the sugar beets and e x p r e s s i n g

RESIDENCE OF A. O. PACKARD.

the juice which is pumped through a pipe line to Lehi. The plant cost about $225,000 and employs about forty persons which makes it an inportant acquisition to the industries of our city.

This autumn there were two tickets in the field for the people's support—The "Progressive Citizen's" ticket, the supporters of which were in favor of selling the Big city pasture, in 5-acre plats, to our young men, who were not land owners, on five years time and at low interest; the money to be expended for electric lights and water works. The remainder of the pasture to be put into the best possible shape for pasturage, and only those who owned no pasture would be permitted to pasture milch cows, only, thereon, at a fair compensation, and all widows to have their cows pastured free. The "People's Party" were in favor of retaining the pasture as it had been—for the pasturage of the cows of the general public. A very spirited campaign was inaugurated and carried on, culminating in a stirring debate in the L. D. S. meeting house, between D. C. Johnson and R. Leo Bird, for the sale; and Thomas Dallin, John S. Boyer and Ernest M. Boyer, against it. On election day the People's Party was victorious by an

overwhelming majority, with the following result: Mayor—Mont Johnson. Councilmen—Ernest M. Boyer, Benjamin T. Blanchard, T. E. Child, Abner Thorn and Hyram Clyde. Recorder—John S. Groesbeck. Treasurer—Thos. Loynd. Marshal—F. C. Gemmell. O. B. Huntington was appointed watermaster and Samuel R. Thurman, city attorney.

In the spring of 1900, George E. Anderson was appointed Bishop of the Second Ward, vice Loren H. Harmer, resigned, with Philip H. Boyer and S. E. Dalton as counselors.

In the latter days of April and the early days of May, there came a terrible calamity upon several families of Springville, which sent a thrill of sorrow and sympathy throughout the entire city—William Konold was killed in a railway accident, on the 24th day of April, at the Cement works, Salt Lake City. It was the same old story—an open switch and the train men thinking they would be back in time to close it. He was brought to Springville, where he had resided, for interment. His funeral was attended by many hundreds of people, by whom he was highly respected. He was a Canadian by birth; 41 years of age, and had been in the employ of the Rio Grande Western railroad for several years. as one of their most trusted employees.

On the first of May. the explosion at Scofield deprived us of Wm. B. Dougall. and John. William and Morgan Miller. On Friday. May 4th. the former was interred. after imposing ceremonies at the L. D. S. meeting house. On Saturday. the 5th. at 10 o'clock. a. m..the obsequies of John Davis and his two sons. who were brought to Springville from Scofield. were held at the L. D. S. meeting house and at 2 o' clock. p. m.. the last rites were performed over the Miller brothers. at the same place.

Never was the entire public heart stirred to such a profound depth as on this occassion. Every person in the city seemed to take a personal interest in trying to alleviate the sorrow that had fallen on the bereaved families.

This fiftieth year has been very dry. less snow and rain having fallen than in any previous year within the memory of the oldest inhabitant. in consequence. many thousand dollars worth of crops will be lost to the farmers and only about three-fourths of a crop will be harvested.

CHAPTER XXI.

WE now come to the Jubilee day. and nearing the completion of our history. Jubilee day opened at the call of fifty guns. at daybreak. and dawned clear and cool. After sunrise the Maccabee band serenaded the city and at 10:30 o'clock. a. m.. an immense audience assembled at the L. D. S. meetinghouse and were called to order by Jas. E. Hall. master of ceremonies. The band played the opening piece after which the choir sang a song composed for the occasion by Wm. Clegg. "Springville's Jubilee." The chaplain. A. J. Southwick. offered the invocation.

The first address was by Mayor Mont Johnson. who spoke briefly of the day that marked an epoch in the history of Springville and its founders. and the band followed with a musical selection.

James E. Hall gave a short but heartfelt speech of welcome. Misses Mattie and Zilla Brown. rendered a duett in a

RESIDENCE OF HENRY MENERAY

charming manner. A response to the speech of welcome was delivered by Ben T. Blanchard. and was rich and racy with incidents of the early day. The Mandolin club. Miss Della Huntington. Chas. Daley and Adelbert Thorn. gave a musical selection which was encored. D. C. Johnson gave reminiscences of the building of Springvile: the Indian wars. and briefly paid tribute to the old-timers. Julia A. Boyer told how the girls performed their various tasks in the household. fifty years ago. Prof. E. Eggertson paid a glowing tribute to the pioneers. in a short. spirited address. Miss Della Huntington and Chas. Daley then gave a mandolin selection. Aaron Johnson. in costume. delivered a humorous address. as an old-timer. which contained many local hits that were well received by the audience.

After dismissal the vast audience adjourned to City Hall park for a public dinner and barbecue. A huge ox had been barbecued to perfection. under the direction of R. L. Bird, chief of committee. Bushels of potatoes had also been beautifully baked. under the direction of Seymour Mendenhall. Each family furnished the sundries. and all partook of a feast spread upon the grass and under the greenwood trees. that was seldom equaled. Thousands were regaled at the feast and a squad of the natives of the valley was fed on the wreck of the spread. as in "ye olden time." The day was an ideal one for a picnic: the air was cool and bracing and the surrounding mountains wore their rich colors of scarlet and gold.

The concluding exercises in the afternoon. were held in the park. a platform had been erected for that purpose in front of the City hall. The program was as follows:

Wand drill. by the public schools. under the direction of Miss Julia Alleman. Hoop drill. under the direction of Miss Hattie Wheeler. May Pole drill. under the direction of Miss Nellie Reynolds. Flag drill. under the direction of Mrs. Rena Roylance. Speech. by Bishop Geo. R. Hill. Reminiscences. "The Black Hawk War." Edwin Lee. Remarks. "Walker War." Ben T. Blanchard. Sentiment. "The Minute Men." Thos. L. Mendenhall. "Young's Express." Geo. McKinzie. "The Star Spangled Banner." by the public schools. under the direction of Aaron Roylance. Comic recitation. by Erastus Z. Clark. Wm. Clegg read an original poem. for which he was awarded the first prize. a beautiful rocking chair. Mrs. Elizabeth Gainge received the second prize for original poem— $2.50. Mrs. Semira Wood. recited with dramatic fire. "Eliza." and Mrs. G. B. Matson. an old-time actress. recited "Flying Jim." in a pleasing and entertaining manner and their prizes were a beautiful cracker jar. each. H. L. Commings read an original poem. by Geo. McKinzie. on the pioneers.

All the pioneers of Springville. who came in the year of 1850. were then presented with a silk badge. after which they gathered at the old cottonwood tree that had spread its shade long before the advent of the pioneer. and had their pictures taken. in a group. by Geo. Anderson. The names of the survivors of 1850. present. were:

Mrs. Eliza Deal. Mrs. Laura Bird. Amos S. Warren. Mrs. Eliza Mendenhall. Cyrus Sanford. Henry Roylance. Wm. Roylance. Frances Nelson. Mrs. Emma Roylance. Alma Roylance. J. P. Humphrey. Leroy Bird. D. C. Johnson. Julia A. Boyer. M. E. Crandall. Melissa Messenger. Wm. Smith and wife. Mrs. Mary B. Mendenhall. Alma Spafford. Willis K. Johnson. Mrs. Zebina Alleman. Ben T. Blanchard. Mrs. Marilla Daniels. Mrs. Tryphena Whitney. Mrs. Mary A. Johnson.

The Utah pioneers who were present were: Geo. R. Hill. Levi N. Kendall. Mrs. Annie Houtz and Geo. B. Matson. The exercises of the day concluded with a most enjoyable ball at Reynold's hall, and a concert at the meeting house. Altogether the day was voted a complete success.

* * *

Thus have passed fifty years with their sunshine and shadow; their toils and hardships and their many compensations. The growth of our city has been slow, but it is progressing more rapidly as the years advance. The optimistic among our inhabitants look hopefully forward to the time when Springville will become one of the model cities of our fair state, with all its resources developed; when the tireless waters of the hills shall be hooked to the wheels of progress; when the pure water shall lie concealed in every street and conducted into every home, affording power and pure beverage in abundance; and by touching a button the lights will flash to illuminate our streets, homes and public halls. And, finally, beauty shall smile on every side, and the deadly malaria, through scientific appliances, shall be banished from our borders, to plague us no more. Vale, fifty years! What of the future? Let the historian of the completed Century record.

BIOGRAPHICAL.

WILLIAM MENDENHALL.

William Mendenhall was born in Mill-hundred, New Castle county, Delaware. and came to Utah and Springville in the autumn of 1852. Immediately upon his arrival he took up his trowel. the use of which he had learned in his native state, and laid the adobes for the houses of Jos. Kelly and Ransom Potter, himself living in one of the rooms of the old fort during the winter. He was identified with the first Sunday school, in 1853, which discontinued during the progress of the Walker war. but resumed his work as a Sunday school teacher, subsequently, which he continued nobly for many years. He was ever found at his post of duty: as guard of the fort during the early Indian troubles. and in the execution of all public duties., He served the city as councilman and held many positions of trust in the branch.

***

WILLIAM WORDSWORTH.

William Wordsworth. one of Utah's pioneers, came to reside at Springville in 1858. He came through the place where Springville now stands. in 1849. in Parley P. Pratt's exploring expedition. He held the office of mayor in

our municipality also that of alderman. He was a man of strong physical frame. blunt and outspoken in his opinions. He was a hard worker and made a full hand at all public work incident to starting a colony in a desert land. He died at Springville. January 10th. 1888.

***

CYRUS SANFORD.

Cyrus Sanford was born in Vermont in 1813. He came to Springville in November. 1850. where he. resided until his death which occurred on the 16th day of May, 1900. He was full of energy and good works all through life. In the early days he was captain of a cavalry company that served in the Walker war. under Colonel John S. Fullmer. and went to relieve the Hand Cart company. in 1856. and returned with his feet badly frozen. He served as councilman and mayor. As latter officer he entered the city plat at the United States land office.

***

WILLIAM CLEGG.

William Clegg. our local poet. arrived in Utah in the year 1864. He was a file cutter by trade. in his native England. He moved to Springville. April 12th.

BARBER SHOP OF HENRY WOOD.

1864. and from that time has labored at whatever his hands found to do. He was a member of the Home guard during the Black Hawk war of 1866-7. He is a gentleman of culture and is much beloved by all who know him.

* *

JAMES E. HALL.

James E. Hall was born at Provo, Utah. October 10th, 1850. and came to live at Springville, with his parents, the next year. His early life was spent at the various labors that engaged the attention of the pioneer boy and attending the village schools in winter. As a man he has been one of the foremost citizens in the development of our city in all lines of advancement. He is a man full of philanthropy and can often be found at the bedside of the afflicted. He has served the city as marshal and mayor and is now a counselor to Bishop Joseph Loynd.

* *

JOHN TUCKET.

John Tucket was selected to preside over the First Ward as Bishop. April 17th, 1892. He has long been a resident of our city and an active man along many industrial lines, also taking a leading part in mutual improvement and Sunday school work. He now follows farming for a livelihood. He was a native of England, but has passed the greater part of his life in Utah

BISHOP GEO. R. HILL.

Bishop Geo. R. Hill was born at Mt. Pisgah, Iowa, August 22nd, 1846, and crossed the plains, with his parents, in a lumber wagon, in A. O. Smoot's company arriving at Salt Lake City, September 22nd, 1847. He lived in Odgen, Utah, until March 26th, 1890, when he secured a residence here. He was appointed Bishop of the Third Ward, April 17th, 1892, which office he now holds. He is a farmer by occupation, but spends much of his time in visiting the poor and lowly and especially those who are sick and afflicted.

* * *

TRYPHENA CRANDALL.

Tryphena Crandall, wife of Myron N. Crandall, was born in New York in 1819, and was married in Nauvoo, Ill. in 1840. She left Nauvoo in 1846, at the time of the general exodus of the Latter Day Saints and sojourned at Kanesville, Iowa, until 1850, when she came to Utah with her husband. She died in the year 1863. Mrs. Crandall was a typical pioneer woman and set an example, in the early days, in frugality and industry that was most admirable.

* * *

DR. FREDERICK DUNN.

Dr. Frederick Dunn was born in Illinois in the year 1864. He received his schooling in the public schools and graduated at the high school of Perry, his native town. At the age of sixteen he commenced to teach school and continued for one year. He took a course in medicine at the Rush medical college, Chicago, where he graduated in 1885, and commenced the practice of his professsion, in Council Grove, Kansas. In 1890 he came to Salt Lake City and remained one year, coming from thence to Springville in 1891 where he has since resided and has acquired a good practice as a physician.

MYRON N. CRANDALL.

Myron N. Crandall was born in the state of New York in 1818. He crossed the plains in 1850 and came to Springville to live, with the first company. He was one of the first counselors to Bishop Johnson and was one of the first aldermen elected in the city, serving in that capacity until 1857. He was one of the noted "Kolob boys." He was a farmer by occupation and died in 1860. During the stirring times of the first decade of Springville's existence, he was a wide-a-wake man and a defender and builder of the new city.

* * *

JAMES WHITEHEAD.

James Whitehead came to the United States from England where he was born over sixty years ago, settling first in Philadelphia. In 1876 he came to reside in Springville, having purchased the woolen mill on Spring creek, which he has since operated. He has labored assiduously to keep home manufacture to the front, being an expert spinner, weaver and dyer. He has served the city as councilman; was called to be counselor to Bishop Packard and for some time was superintendent of the Springville Sunday school.

* * *

EDWIN WHITING.

Edwin Whiting was born in Massachusetts, September 9th, 1809. Though not a pioneer of Springville, he passed through here in 1849, with the colony that settled at Manti. He came to reside at Springville in the year 1861 and his coming marked an era in the culture of finer fruits and ornamental shade trees. He gave impetus to the trans-planting of the evergreen from its native haunts in the mountains, to our city. He was a lover of nature and his long, busy life, was devoted to "making glad the waste places." He died at Mapleton, December 7th, 1890.

WILLIAM M. ROYLANCE.

William M. Roylance is a Springville born citizen, who has made the most of his opportunities and forged to the front in a most successful manner, as produce merchant, and politician. He attended the public schools of the city and while yet in his 'teens learned telegraphy and the routine of railway office work. Soon after attaining his majority, he engaged in the produce shipping business which he has continued with varying success, to its present proportions. In 1891-4 he was elected to hold a councilman's chair in the city council. In 1896 he was elected as a member of the legislature and also in 1898, at which term he was chosen speaker. In the latter year he moved to Provo, where he proposes to make his future home.

**

DORR P. CURTIS.

Dorr P. Curtis came to Springville during the "move" of 1858. He served one term as city councilor and for some years was counselor to Bishop Johnson and was a very active man in military affairs in the Utah militia, having been commissioned colonel by the governor. He moved from Springville some years ago and now lives at Oakley, Idaho. He was born in New York in 1819.

**

GEORGE A. STORRS.

George A. Storrs, is a Springville boy, who was educated here: in the district schools and spent his time at the various labors of farming and railroad grading, etc. until the autumn of 1893, when he was elected on the Democratic ticket as city marshal, which position he filled with fidelity and trust until 1897, when he was elected to the office of sheriff of the county, which office he now holds. As marshal and sheriff he has shown commendable skill as a detective officer.

BENJAMIN T. BLANCHARD.

Benjamin T. Blanchard was a boy of 12 years of age when he came with his parents to Springville. Since then he has been one of the active workers of the town, as Indian interpreter, Bishop's counselor, Sunday school teacher and city councilor. He is a farmer by occupation, but finds much time to devote to the spiritual and social advancement of the ward, and is at present a member of the city council.

**

DAVIS CLARK.

Davis Clark came to live in Springville in the year 1852, and since that time has resided here. He was one of the most active of the pioneers, in subduing the wilderness and in assisting to keep the savages at bay in the various Indian wars. He was a part owner in the first steam sawmill that came to our city. Every canyon and timber slide in our vicinity bears the marks of his ax. He has been engaged in farming and fruit raising, for the last ten years and is a man full of tireless energy and enterprise. He is a native of Connecticut.

**

LYMAN S. WOOD.

Lyman S. Wood, the first recorder of our city, was born in Ohio, sixty-eight years ago and came to Salt Lake City in September 1848. His first labor in the mountains was making adobes for his parents home. At the beginning of 1849 he taught school at Big Cottonwood and in the winter of 1850, at Salt Lake City. In February, 1853, he came to Springville, where he has since resided. During the early years he came in contact with the Indians almost daily and became well acquainted with their character and habits and well versed in their language. He was connected with Indian affairs during the early years and probably understands the traditions and peculiarities of the

Lamanites as well as any person in the state. He was elected alderman of the city in 1861, and from 1863 to 1889, he served the city as mayor, without receiving a single dollar as salary. Mr. Wood was elected to serve two terms in the legislature.

JOHN ROYLANCE.

John Roylance emigrated from England to the United States when a young man. He was a member of the "Mormon Battalion," and came to Springville to live the first year of its settlement. He was a steady-going man, honest and industrious and spent his time mostly on the farm, in which he took great delight. He was one of the first directors of the Co-op and proved a a sagacious and entirely trustworthy man.

GEORGE E. ANDERSON.

George E. Anderson was born in Salt Lake City, where he grew to manhood. In his early 'teens he herded cows "over Jordan," during the summer and attended school in the winter. He worked with C. R. Savage for several years, learning the art of photography. He established a gallery at Manti in the eighties and located in Springville about the year 1890. He was appointed Bishop of the Second Ward, vice Loren Harmer, resigned. He is a promoter of art studies and a busy worker in the Mutual Improvement association and Sunday school.

LOREN HARMER.

Loren Harmer is a native of Springville and received the appointment of Bishop of the Second Ward the 17th of April 1892. He has followed farming as an occupation since he was large enough to make a harvest hand and is still engaged as a husbandman.

GEORGE H. MAYCOCK.

George H. Maycock was appointed to succeed John Tucket, resigned, as Bishop of the First Ward. He is a native of our city and one or our leading farmers.

JACOB HOUTZ.

Jacob Houtz was the first projector and builder of the gristmill on Spring creek, in 1851-2, and afterwards built a new mill on the site of the old one. He was one of the original company to build the woolen factory, on Spring creek, in the early sixties. He was at one time a merchant, in company with Wm. Bringhurst, their store being situated on Spring creek, where they did an extensive barter with the "cotton country" people for their chief staple that was put into the various domestic fabrics at their factory. Mr. Houtz was a man of untiring industry, pluck and energy.

DON C. JOHNSON.

GIDEON D. WOOD.

Gideon D. Wood, is a native of New York. having been born there in 1808. He emigrated to the Salt Lake valley in 1858. He was sent to Parowan to assist in planting a colony there. returning to Salt Lake in May, and moved to Springville in the autumn of 1852. At an early day he went into the mercantile business. He was the first chief executive of our municipality and served as alderman and two terms as city councilor. He was a successful farmer and stock raiser. Many hearts were made glad by his timely advice and philanthrophy. He was a devoted Christian and well respected by all who knew him. He passed to his final reward on the 9th day of September. 1890.

***

SOLOMON CHASE.

Solomon Chase came with the exodus of 1858 to reside in Springville. He early took the contract. in partnership with John Metcalf. to finish the inside of the Big school house. They subsequently changed it to its present dimensions and since that time it has served as the L. D. S. church. He was one of our leading mechanics. and his handiwork is upon many of the dwellings of the city. He served as city councilor and was one of the counselors of Wm. Bringhurst during his incumbency of the bishopric.

***

ALEXANDER F. MACDONALD.

Alexander F. Macdonald. the third mayor of Springville. was born in Rosshire. Scotland. September 11th. 1825, and came to Salt Lake City October 2nd. 1854, and came to Springville in the following December to work for Jacob Houtz. upon the gristmill then in course of repair. He acted as Bishop Johnson's clerk for some years. For the last ten years he has resided in Mexico.

H. M. DOUGALL.

H. M. Dougall came to Springville. with his widowed mother, in 1856, direct from England. He has been known as a freighter and railroad contractor, before the advent of the railway. in 1868, and as sawmill and gristmill owner in the more recent times. all of which business prospered under his management. In the late years he has been mostly engaged in ranching. stock raising and merchandising. He being a partner in the firm of the G. S. Wood Mercantile company. He was sent to the legislature by the voters of Utah county. in 1894. He has filled the office of city councilor and postmaster and is at this time deputy postmaster.

***

NEPHI PACKARD.

Nephi Packard was the third Bishop of Springville Ward. He came here. with his parents. in 1851. and was one of the "boys" in the early rustling. necessary to keep things properly in hand; being engaged in all the road and canal building and Indian fighting. In 1860. in connection with Henry Moesser, he established the first book store in our town. in the annex to the little hall which he had built that year. He crossed the plains to the Missouri river as a freighter of merchandise. in the sixties. He was appointed Bishop of Springville in 1883 and served until 1893. For the last few years he has been engaged in prospecting and mining. being a very skillful assayer.

***

DR. GEORGE SMART.

Dr. George Smart was born in England in 1863 and came to Provo. with his parents. in 1874. His education was received at the public schools and Brigham Young academy. at Provo. He began his medical studies in 1885. at the Ohio Medical college and graduated in 1889. He began practice at Provo and was appointed city physician in 1892. In 1893-4, he took a post graduate course and was the first to introduce the asceptic, or new surgery, and diptheria anti-toxine into Utah county. He moved to Springville in 1896, where by his skill and industry he has acquired a large practice.

EDWIN LEE.

Edwin Lee was born in England in 1831 and came to reside in our city in October 12th, 1854. Since that time, he has been full of life and energy, as a public servant and as a Tintic war soldier and in the Black Hawk war. For many years he has been head water-master and there is, probably, not a man in our city who understands the water rights of the people better than Edwin Lee.

∗

LORENZO JOHNSON.

Lorenzo Johnson was elected mayor for the years 1859-61; he had previously served the city as councilman two terms. Mr. Johnson arrived in Springville with his family in the year of 1852, and remained here for twelve years, when he was called, in connection with others, to go into Southern Utah to colonize on the Muddy River. There his health failed and he removed to Monroe, Sevier Co., where he made a home, dying there April 26, 1872. He was one of those who opened Big Cottonwood canyon, and helped to build the several sawmills there in the early '50s. Mr. Johnson was born in Connecticut April 17. 1813.

∗

DR. C. J. PETERSON,

Dr. C. J. Peterson was born in Copenhagen, Denmark, in 1862. Graduated from the Royal seminary at Jalling in 1878. Took the degree Artium the same year and was admitted to the Royal university at Copenhagen. Received the degree Cand. Phil., 1879.

Took up the study of medicine and graduated from the Medical Theoretical department, 1884. Emigrated to America the same year; took a course in medicine at the College of Physicians and Surgeons. and at Bennett's Medical college both at Chicago. Engaged in the drug business at Springville in 1890. From 1891-3 he served the city as quarantine physician. He is a skillful druggist and is doing a thriving business in that line.

∗

WILLIAM D. JOHNSON

William D. Johnson was a young man of about 19 years of age when he arrived at Springville in 1852. and became a participant in the early Indian difficulties. He was a member of the party that went to build Fort Supply in 1856, commanded a platoon in the Echo war of '57. and was a member of the Kolob party in 1859. Mr. Johnson assisted Nelson Spafford in constructing the first timber bridge across Hobble Creek; was one of the first to open up the right hand fork of Hobble Creek canyon and to build the sawmill in that locality. He was elected city marshal in '59 and afterwards served as councilman. About the year 1880. he emigrated to Arizona where he now resides, and serves as counselor to the Stake presidency.

JOSEPH LOYND.

Joseph Loynd is a native of England. who was born in the year 1843. and left his childhood home May 25, 1856. for the land of Zion. He pulled a hand cart across the plains and arrived in Salt Lake City, Nov. 30. Mr. Loynd came to reside in Springville in the year of the "move." In 1864 he drove one of the Springville 8-ox-teams to the Missouri river and back for the Mormon emigration of that year. He knows from actual experience the trials and vicissitudes of early pioneer life: he is a farmer by profession, has been a member of the City council, and in 1892 was appointed to preside over the Fourth ward as b'sh'p.

⁎

CYRUS E. DALLIN.

Cyrus Edwin Dallin was born in this city on Nov. 22, 1861, where he resided until 1880, when he went to Boston and entered the studio of Truman H. Bartlett, the sculptor, and began his art studies. His nineteen years of boy life in Springville were not unlike those of the majority of the village boys of that period, being spent in herding cows, fishing, hunting, going to the canyons for wood, picking the wild berries, rolling rocks down the steep mountain sides, and exploring the caverns; attending the village schools during the inclement season, where he was known as a local artist of no mean ability, as the numerous sketches on fences and walls would indicate. When about fourteen years of age he did some produce peddling at Alta City in Little Cottonwood canyon. In the spring of 1879 he went to work at a mine in the Tintic district, in the dual capacity of cook and sorter of ores. It was while at work in this mine that a vein of white clay was struck, and out of which the sculptor boy carved two heads that gave him local notice and resulted in an exhibition of his handiwork at the Territorial Fair of 1879. At Boston, and later on at Paris, his genius quickly made him famous, and he now ranks among the foremost sculptors of the age. He has been awarded a great many prizes for the originality and artistic excellence of his work. As a man Mr. Dallin has ever remained one of the people, whole-souled and genial, and totally unspoiled by the plaudits of the artistic world.

Mr. Dallin has returned to his native town several times in the last twenty years, where his heart seems centered though he still resides in Boston. His last work this year was to finish the Pioneer statue of Brigham Young, which was completed on the 24th of July.

⁎

JOHN S. BOYER.

John S. Boyer came to live in Springville in 1854, and hired out as a cow

PROF. LARS E. EGGERTSON.

herder for the summer, living with Wm. Huggins and returning to Salt Lake for the winter months. The next spring he came back and worked for his uncle Jacob Houtz, doing farm work and stints on the fort wall, returning to Salt Lake City and attending

RESIDENCE OF L. D. DEAL.

school during the winter. In the spring of 1856 he came to live at Springville permanently, where he has followed the avocations of freighter and farmer. He was elected justice of the peace in 1874, which office he has held continuously until Jan. 1, 1900. From the numerous appeals taken from his court none of his decisions have been set aside. He was chosen as delegate to attend the Territorial convention of 1882 to frame a State constitution and also in '95 to frame the present State constitution. He is a Pennsylvanian by birth, and was born Dec. 7, 1840.

***

WILLIAM M. BROMLEY.

William Michael Bromley was born in England, October 13, 1839, and came to America with his parents in 1851, locating at St. Louis, Mo., and came to Utah in '55; he drove six yoke of oxen across the plains, arriving at Salt Lake City late in the autumn. He walked from there to this city, arriving on December 7th. Mr. Bromley passed through the rigors of the grasshopper war, not tasting bread for months, but subsisting upon fish, roots, greens, etc.

He assisted in all the public improvements in the early days; was a member of the brass band of '58 and was its leader in '61; was appointed captain of Company A, Second regiment, Utah militia, by Gov. Doty, and was actively engaged during the Black Hawk war. He was one of the pioneer movers in Y. M. M. I. A. work, and acted as counselor to Bishops Johnson and Bringhurst. Mr. Bromley went on a mission to England in 1870, presiding over the Bristol conference, and to New Zealand in 1880, acting as president. In '83 he was appointed bishop of American Fork. He held successively the offices of city marshal, recorder, councilor and justice. By trade he was a blacksmith.

***

GEORGE HARRISON

George Harrison, who for the last twenty-five years has been the ward chorister, was born in England and emigrated to the United States with his parents in 1856. He started upon the arduous hand-cart journey the same autumn and endured all the trials and hardships incident to that fatal journey. For the want of provisions he was glad to eat the rawhide with which the old carts were mended, and could not even get enough of this loathsome food to allay the cravings of hunger. One day he went into an Indian tepee wherein a large pot of juicy venison was cooking. He pointed to the pot and then to his mouth. The squaw in charge understood and fed the famished youth several pounds, but was compelled to desist for fear of killing him on the spot. Mr. Harrison came to Springville to live in 1858, and was one of the Black Hawk volunteers. For the last twenty years he has kept an hotel, and has became known far and wide as a prime cook and an all round genial gentleman.

.

WILLIAM T. TEW.

William Thomas Tew was born in the city of Springville on the 2nd day of February, 1859. When six years old he moved with his parents to Idaho, returning to Springville in 1872. After his return he worked at the mason's trade for a few years and then moved to Mapleton, where he followed the occupation of a farmer. He was an active member of the M. I. A. and held the office of president; he was also an industrious worker in the Sunday Schools. Mr. Tew was ordained as bishop of Mapleton, May 19, 1896.

.

JAMES OAKLEY.

James Oakley was born on Long Island, New York, Sept. 5, 1826, and moved to Nauvoo, Ill., while he was quite young, and where he acquired most of his schooling. In 1846 he was called as a member of the Mormon Battalion and made the march to Santa Fe, where he was left upon the sick list. From Pueblo he traveled to Fort Laramie, where he obtained a furlough and overtook the pioneer band at Green river. He came to reside at Spring-

ville at an early day and has been closely identified with all the public labors. Mr. Oakley was chief mason at the laying of the foundation of the meeting house, and later went out to assist in building Fort Supply. He was an active member of the "Y. X. Company," and served the city two years as councilor.

.

EMELINE C. BIRD.

Emeline Crandall Bird, consort of Richard Bird, came to Springville to reside Oct. 1st, 1850. She was one of the queens of the household, and by deftness and industry, spun and wove the fabrics composing the wardrobe of her husband and children. She was born in New York, and died at Springville in 1899.

.

JOSEPH W. BISSELL.

Joseph W. Bissell is a native of Boston, where he lived until early manhood, when he emigrated to Utah, arriving in Springville in 1852. He saw some hard times during the '50s in this state. Early in the '60s he made several trips north into Montana, and was quite successful. For many years he was engaged in mercantile pursuits, and acted for some years as superintendent of the Springville Co-op. Mr. Bissell served the city as justice of the peace and treasurer several terms.

.

FREDERICK WEIGHT.

Frederick Weight has been one of the most useful citizens of our little commonwealth as laborer and chorister. Not only did he find time aside from his labors as plasterer to make and repair musical instruments, but to give instructions in the musical art during the early years of the settlement's growth. For many years he was chorister and brought the choir, through most indefatigable labors to a high state of proficiency. For the last ten years he has presided at the organ under the leadership of Chorister Harrison. He arrived in Springville in 1856 and became a permanent resident. In November, 1856, he was appointed a teacher in the Sunday School and choir leader, by Bishop Johnson, which positions he held for twenty-four years. In 1865 he was appointed drum major by Col. Wm. Bromley, and was one of the Home Guard during the Indian wars of '66–7.

.

JUTATHAN AVERETT.

Jutathan Averett, one of the Mormon Battalion, came to Utah in 1852, and to Springville to live on Christmas, 1857. He was born in Alabama 86 years ago, and has always been known as a quiet, busy man. During the last few years he has been quite hard of hearing and nearly blind.

.

ABRAM NOE.

Abram Noe who for many years was connected with the city council and held the office of justice of the peace, was born in Cincinnati, Ohio, Dec. 18, 1820. At an early age he learned the trade of silversmith. He came to reside in Springville in the year of '58 and has since resided here. For many years he worked in connection with Newman Bulkley in opening roads into the canyons. He took a prominent part in the early Y. M. M. I. A. and assisted very materially in building it to a point of great excellence.

.

WILLIAM MILLER.

William Miller is really entitled to the honor of locating Springville as a townsite. He came to Utah in 1849, and first located and built a home in Salt Lake City. In 1855 he was elected

mayor of Springville, serving for two years. Mr. Miller chose the site of the present Tithing office as a home lot, and in 1859 built around it a fine stone wall. In 1860 he was called to go to Provo to preside as bishop. He was born in the state of New York in the year 1814, and died at Provo in 1875.

Pheobe Scott Miller, his wife, was born in his native state, and was by his side in all their early wanderings connected with the L. D. S. church. She was one of the first school teachers in the old fort. Her death occured in 1855.

.

RICHARD BIRD.

Richard Bird, one of the first to arrive at Springville in 1850, commenced his mundane career in the Empire state. Oct. 13. 1820. He settled in Far West. Mo., Nauvoo. Ill., and Iowa, and came to Springville Oct. 1st, 1850. He held the office of constable for many years, was an active man in

WILLIAM F. GIBSON.

all military matters and Indian wars of the early days, holding the position of aide-de-camp on Maj. Gen. Johnson's staff. He was a man of untiring industry and a farmer by profession.

* *

THOMAS CHILD.

Thomas Child, the subject of this sketch, was born near Bradford. Yorkshire, England. February 11, 1825, came to Utah on Sept. 3rd, 1852, and moved to Springville in 1856. During all his life he has been a busy worker at the mason's trade, and also in the duty of his office of head teacher, which he held for many years. The teams sent from Springville to haul rock for the Salt Lake Temple and to transport the poor Saints across the plains from the Missouri river, were raised and fitted out under his supervision. He has collected thousands of dollars for various public enterprises. In short, Thomas Child never learned the word fail.

* *

MARTIN P. CRANDALL.

M. P. Crandall, one of the Pioneers of Springville, was born in New York, Oct. 7th, 1830. He was an active participant in the early Indian wars, was a member of the rescue party sent out to relieve the hand cart company in 1856 and of the "Y. X. Company" in 1857. He was one of the early freighters to California, Montana and to Missouri River points. During his entire life he was a stirring, industrious man.

* *

MILAN PACKARD.

Milan Packard, one of our capitalists, has resided in Springville since the autumn of 1851 and has been closely identified with the material interests of our growing city all the fifty years of its existence. As an early freighter to the Missouri river points. Montana and California, he began to acquire the means that has made him a successful merchant, stock and sheep man, local banker and miner. He is tireless in his labors and has been one of the foremost workers in our city in advocating public improvements.

* *

ELIZA DEAL.

Eliza Crandall married John W. Deal at Quincy, Ill., and accompanied her husband throughout their early journeys to the land of Zion. She is well versed in the early history of our city, having had a hand in all the early labors of providing "home spun" for the members of her family. She was born in "York State" in the year 1828, and still enjoys life surrounded by her numerous children and grandchildren.

* *

NOAH T. GUYMON.

Noah T. Guymon began this life in North Carolina in the year 1818. He came to Springville to live in the autumn of 1851 and for ten years was a counselor to Bishop Johnson; he also held several important county and city offices. Mr. Guymon took an active part in all the early Indian troubles and in works of a public nature. At the present time he resides in Castle Valley, Utah.

* *

GEORGE B. MATSON.

George B. Matson came to reside in Springville in February, 1854, and has been closely identified with its interests all the years since. He passed through this vicinity in the autumn of 1849 in company with Parley Pratt and went as far south as St. George. On Christmas day, 1850, he assisted in raising the first liberty pole at Parowan. In 1856 he went with the relief teams as far as Fort Bridger to assist the belated handcart company, and was a member of the "Y. X. Company" in '57. Mr. Matson was first introduced to the scenes of this life on the 26th day of October, 1827, in the State of Delaware. He lived at Nauvoo. Ill., and was as a boy a member at one time of Joseph Smith's household. Came to Utah about Oct. 1st, 1847. In his youth he learned the brick mason's trade and his trowel rang upon many of the first buildings in Salt Lake City and also in Springville. In the later years farming has occupied most of his time.

_

WILLIAM SUMSION.

William Sumsion came to Springville from England with his parents at an early day. He was early identified with the threshing machine interests, and later became a railway construction contractor. For ten years he was the superintendent of the Springville Sunday Schools, and under his supervision it was a very superior organization. For the last few years he has been engaged in railway work and mining.

_

L. J. WHITNEY.

L. J. Whitney, a Union soldier, became a resident of Springville in 1865 and built a Government sawmill in Strawberry valley, where much of our finishing lumber came from—including that for the meeting house. In 1866 he was one of the Minute men and bivouacked at the Tithing corral with the boys, whom he used to drill in cavalry tactics on Saturday afternoons. He was one of the original owners of the Sunbeam mine at Tintic and of late years has followed mining.

_

JOHN W. DEAL.

John W. Deal was a native of North Carolina, where he was born in 1822, and his early life was spent upon the Mississippi river as a flatboatman. His was one among the original ten wagons arriving at Springville. He was a farmer during his residence here; but at odd times he was engaged in brick-making, he having made the first brick in town; he was also the original lime burner of the city. His trade was that of stone cutter, which trade he plied at Nauvoo in dressing rock for its Temple. Mr. Deal was a man of infinite jest and good humor.

_

MARY A. JOHNSON.

Mary A. Johnson, second wife of Aaron Johnson, was one of the early tireless, energetic spirits of the pioneer town. She handled the tithing for many years as clerk and was frequently referred to as Bishop Johnson's "right hand man." Though the mother of a large family, she took an unselfish part in the arduous labors of her husband's household and in looking after the poor of the ward. In 1888 she removed from Springville with her family and for the last ten years has lived at Bancroft, Idaho. She was born in New York, Aug. 3, 1831.

_

JANE SCOTT JOHNSON.

Jane S. Johnson, one of the pioneer women of this city. was born in Livingston county, N. Y.. July 10, 1822. She was a school teacher at her native home, from which she emigrated to Nauvoo in 1844, coming nearly the entire distance on a lumber raft and sailing upon the Alleghany, Ohio and Mississippi rivers. She taught a private school in Springville for some years in the early times, in which were taught Bishop Johnson's children and some of those of the near neighborhood.

_

EDWIN LUCIUS WHITING.

Edwin Lucius Whiting was the first bishop of Mapleton. That ward was, until the spring of 1900, within the corporate limits of Springville and indeed seems a part of our city still, for the reason that it was settled by residents of this city and it is hard to separate the Springvillian from the Mapletonian. In 1886, Mapleton was set apart as a separate ecclesiastical ward with Edwin L.

RESIDENCE OF J. M. WESTWOOD.

Whiting as presiding elder and superintendent of the Sunday School. with Wm. T. Tew and John Mendenhall as counselors. Two years later he was ordained bishop of Mapleton ward. with the aforesaid counselors. He took an active part in the Black Hawk war as a minute man of the Home Guard. Mr. Whiting was a tireless. energetic man and much preferred the labors of his farm to those of a public nature. He died Feb. 12. 1896. after a useful life of 51 years.

*
**

EMELINE POTTER MILLER.

Emeline Potter. wife of Wm. Miller. came to this city with the first settlers and for ten years was a resident here. moving to Provo in 1860. where she has since resided. She was the principal weaver in the Miller household. During parts of the first year she and Mrs. Marilla Miller taught school in the village.

*
**

WILLIAM D. HUNTINGTON.

William D. Huntington. the seventh executive of this city, was born in New York in 1818, came to Utah in 1849 and to live in this city in the fall of '51. In 1853 he was called to go upon an ex-

ploring expedition to the Navajo country to seek a place for colonization. He took a great interest in music and the drama in the early day and manufactured the large and small drums used by our brass and martial bands for many years. In 1857 he was selected by Gov. Young to guard the California emigrants safely through the Territory. being empowered to call out the entire militia force if necessary to give them safe escort. He was a fearless. outspoken man and much admired by his friends as ''a prince of good fellows.''

*
**

AMOS S. WARREN.

Amos S. Warren was one of the youngest of the young men who came first to settle Springville and has lived here all the years since. taking an active part in all the early Indian wars and other arduous labors of subduing a new country. His services have been valuable at times as an Indian interpreter. whose dialect he can speak like a native. He has followed the occupation of blacksmith and beekeeper. His brothers William and Charles. at an early day moved to Spanish Fork, where they rendered invaluable aid in building up our sister town,

MARILLA JOHNSON MILLER.

Marilla Johnson. second wife of Wm. Miller. was born in Connecticut and with her parents followed the Mormon people from Kirtland. O., to Nauvoo. Ill.. and through Iowa to Utah in 1849. She was one of the early school teachers of the town, and since moving to Provo in 1860 has successfully managed the Excelsior house—then the leading hostelry. The last ten years she has been connected with the stake presidency of the Relief Society. to the duties of which office she has devoted much of her time.

***

NEWMAN BULKLEY.

Newman Bulkley, a member of the Mormon Battalion, came early to reside in this city and was a hard worker in producing material with which to build dwellings. He. in connection with Abram Noe. opened the "slide"—still bearing his name—north of town, from whence thousands of feet of lumber were procured that entered into the construction of the first houses. He was a mountain worker for years until he became broken down in health. owing to the extreme exposure to the mountain blasts and snow.

***

ALEXANDER ROBERTSON.

Alexander Robertson served Springville as mayor for the years 1889-91, having previously served several terms as councilor. He was born in Forfairshire. Scotland. Aug. 11. 1831. and emigrated to the United States in 1850. and to Utah in 1852. He served in the Tintic war of '56. the Echo war of '57, and came to Springville to live the same winter. before the New Year. Mr. Robertson is by trade a farmer and for the last nine years has acted as agent for the Utah Sugar Company at Springville. and is regarded as an authority on sugar beet culture.

NELSON SPAFFORD.

Nelson Spafford enlisted in the army for the Mexican war and marched to Mexico, where he served under General Scott at the storming of the Capital. He came to Springville with his parents in the autumn of 1850 and married Emma Johnson in the spring of '51. In the early days he took an active part in scouting expeditions incident to the settlement of the new country and was with the party that went to rescue the hand-cart company in the bleak winter of '56. He built the first timber bridge across Hobble creek on the site of the present one. Mr. Spafford moved to Annabella. Sevier county, early in the '70s. where he now resides.

***

LEVI N. KENDALL.

Levi N. Kendall, one of the Utah Pioneers of '47, came to be a citizen of Springville in 1856. Mr. Kendall has assisted in the construction of the canyon roads and irrigating canals and has lead an industrious life. For the last few years he has been a resident of Mapleton. where he is honored each 24th by the citizens of that burg. who are proud of their "old-timer."

***

WILLIAM BRAMALL.

William Bramall is an Englishman and for the Gospel's sake emigrated to Utah and came to reside here in the autumn of '52. When he left Salt Lake City he kept his eyes open for big wheat stacks. thinking such would indicate a good place wherein to set his stakes and grow up with the country. The big stacks of grain loomed up at Springville and our homeseeker said "Whoa!" to the old oxen and here he has lived ever since. He filled two missions to his native country since then and has held several civil and ecclesiastical offices. at one time acting as a counselor to Bishop Johnson.

During the Black Hawk war he had charge of outfitting the men and looking after the families at home. which he did to the entire satisfaction of all parties concerned. He is a farmer by profession and is quoted as an authority on farming matters.

R. A. DEAL.

R. A. Deal, who served as mayor of the city for three terms. was born in Springville. Feb. 3, 1852. where he has since resided. He was educated at the city schools. supplemented by some special courses at various times. Mr. Deal has been a very successful business man as merchant. banker and railway contractor. and has been a leading spirit in the public enterprises of the past decade. He has served as a county commissioner, and in his conduct of public business is known as a careful and progressive man. At present he is extensively engaged in merchandising and railroad contracting.

NOAH PACKARD.

Noah Packard came at the early date of 1851 to reside in Springville. He was one of the eloquent preachers of the early '50s. a man of great piety and scriptural lore. He followed farming as an occupation during his short life in Springville. He was born in Massachusetts in 1800 and died here in 1858.

WM. J. STEWART.

Wm. J. Stewart. the first merchant of Springville. was born in Tennessee. Dec. 19, 1814. came to Utah in 1847, and to Springville in the autumn of 1850. His occupation in life was that of trader and merchant up to the time of his death. which occurred Dec. 5, 1884. He contributed liberally to all the public works of the early days.

LUCIEN D. & NELSON D. CRANDALL.

Lucien D. and Nelson D. Crandall were the youngest of the Crandall brothers. being not yet out of their 'teens when they arrived in Springville with the first squad. They both went to California in the early '50s. where they resided a few years. when Nelson returned to this city where he lived until his demise. Lucien returned some years later and made his home here for a time. subsequently returning to California where he remained until his decease. Nelson was a freighter and railroad contractor most of the busy years of his life.

H. T. REYNOLDS.

H. T. Reynolds was born. grew up and was educated in this city. and since attaining manhood has been active and energetic in all public enterprises. having held the office of city councilor several terms, and also county commissioner one term. He is a successful merchant and has also done a vast amount of railroad contracting. He was appointed superintendent of the Third Ward Sunday school in 1897, which position he still holds. He was 40 years old on the 11th day of March, 1900.

STEPHEN C. PERRY.

Stephen C. Perry was among the early settlers and was known locally as the first chair maker, some of which bear the name of "S. C. Perry. maker," and are still cherished as heirlooms and souvenirs of the pioneer age. He was one of the messengers to make overtures of peace to the hostiles of Walker's band. encamped at Payson canyon, and narrowly escaped losing his scalp at the hands of the blood thirsty savages at that critical time. He was one of our most useful citizens of the early day.

DAVID P. FELT.

David P. Felt was born Aug. 7, 1860, at Salt Lake City and received his education in the public schools. He is a rustler and full of energy in whatever he undertakes. He embarked in the book and stationery business at Provo and conducted the Utah Industrialist for several years; at one time he was president of the Utah Press Association. In 1895 he became owner and editor of The Springville Independent, and in 1897 was called to fill a mission to the Southern States. Mr. Felt now holds a position on the Deseret News.

***

MONTEZUMA JOHNSON.

Montezuma Johnson, the present mayor of Springville, was born in this city about the end of the first decade of its settlement. He was educated in the city schools. and has mostly followed farming as a profession. In November. 1899, he was elected mayor of the city.

***

JOHN W. STREEPER.

John Wilkinson Streeper was troop farrier, in Troop I, Torrey's Rough Riders, recruited for services in Cuba. during the Spanish-American war. He enlisted at Springville on April 30th, 1898, and went to Jacksonville, Fla.. and was mustered out of service on Oct. 27, 1898. Mr. Streeper was educated at the Hungerford academy and has been engaged in stock raising and farming much of his life. He was born in Weber Co.. Utah. Feb. 6. 1872.

***

LARS E. EGGERTSEN.

Lars E. Eggertsen is a Provo boy. having been born there in March. 1866. and obtained his education in the public schools of that city. He graduated at the B. Y. academy in the class of '89

and at the Cleary Business College of Ypsilanti, Mich., in '91. and received the degree of B. Ped. at the B. Y. A. in '95; and a grammar diploma in 1900 from the State Board of Education. In 1899 he read a paper before the National Teachers' association at Los Angeles. being the first Utah boy thus honored. Mr. Eggertsen has been a teacher for twelve years and in the district schools two years, being principal of the Springville schools this year and last. He now holds the office of county superintendent of Sunday Schools for Utah county. He has spent nearly three years in Europe and may be counted as one of our most active and energetic citizens along all progressive lines.

***

ANER HUMPHREY.

Aner Humphrey first saw the light in the city of San Bernardino, Cal., Nov. 10, 1869, and came to live in this city with his parents early in the '70s. He was educated at the Hungerford academy and has been engaged in the various labors of farming. mining. timberman and clerk. Mr. Humphrey enlisted in Battery A. Utah Volunteer Artillery. April 28, 1898. and did faithful and meritorious service in the Philippine campaign.

***

ETHER BLANCHARD.

Ether Blanchard was born in Garden Grove. Iowa, Aug. 16, 1846. and came to Springville with his parents in 1852, where he has since resided. As a member of the Home Guard he did good service in the Black Hawk war. He is a farmer by profession and is considered one of the yeomanry of the city. Mr. Blanchard is also a poet.

***

DON C. FULMER, JR.

Don C. Fullmer, jr., enlisted on the 18th day of May. 1898, in the First Nevada Cavalry for service in the Philippines, and was honorably discharged from the service on Nov. 15th, 1899, after eighteen months arduous service in the far-away islands. He was born, grew up and attended the public schools, in Springville. His labors have been varied, as is common to the young men of our community. Upon his return home, quite unexpected to himself the people gave him a rousing reception.

***

FRANK HARMER.

Frank Harmer is a Springville boy and has resided here the greater part of his life. He acquired a common school education in the district schools. Mr. Harmer enlisted in the Utah batteries on the 28th day of April, 1898, and served in the Philippines in Battery A under Major R. W. Young. For meritorious service he arose to the rank of corporal. He was born Aug. 12, 1876, and is by occupation a farmer.

***

STANLEY STATEN.

Stanley Staten was born in Springville, May 3rd, 1877. He grew to manhood here, assisting his father at the farm work and received his education at the Hungerford academy. On the 28th day of April he enlisted for the Spanish-American war, and served in the Philippines in Battery A under Major Young. He returned to America in August, 1899, and was mustered out on the 16th of that month, returning home on the 19th.

***

MELVIN G. HARMER.

Melvin G. Harmer was born in Springville, Sept. 26, 1877, and received his education in the district schools. He enlisted in Troop C, Eleventh Cavalry, U. S. V., at Salt Lake City on the 21st day of August, 1899, and was assigned to the Philippines, where he participated in the campaign in the southern part of Luzon. He was in

action several times, and was at the battle of Mateo where Gen. Lawton was killed and assisted in carrying his body to the hospital. He was mustered out of service Sept. 14, 1900, on account of sickness.

***

WILLIAM M. TIPTON.

William Morton Tipton, a member of Battery A, Utah Volunteers, was born in Casey, Clark County, Ill., Jan. 6, 1875, and came to Springville with his parents in 1879, where he grew to manhood. He was educated at the Hungerford academy. On April 28, 1898, he enlisted in the Utah batteries and served in the Philippines, returning with his comrades in 1899. He was mustered out of the service on the 16th of August. Since attaining man's estate Mr. Tipton has labored principally as a miner.

***

WILLIAM H. LITER, JR.

William H. Liter, jr., was enlisted to go with Torrey's Rough Riders at this city, on the 30th day of April, 1898, and accompanied the Troop under the command of Capt. John Q. Cannon to Jacksonville, Fla., where he was quartered for several months and served until his muster out, Oct. 27, 1898. Mr. Liter was educated at the Hungerford academy. His birthplace was in Salt Lake City, May 18, 1872. Mr. Liter served as a troop wagoner.

***

WILLIAM B. DOUGALL.

William Bernard Dougall was born in Springville, July 23, 1872. He graduated at the Hungerford academy in this city and at the Agricultural college at Logan. Mr Dougall's profession was that of civil engineer which occupation he followed quite successfully, having attained great proficiency in his chosen profession. At the breaking out of the last war, he offered his services to his country by enlisting in Company K, Second Regiment Volunteer Engineers for service in the Sandwich Islands. on the 9th day of June. 1898. He received the appointment of Sergeant and was afterwards commissioned Lieutenant. Upon his muster out. he resumed the duties of surveyor and was in the employ of the Pleasant Valley Coal Company as such when he met his untimely fate on the fatal 1st day of May. 1900.

***

DON C. JOHNSON. JR.

Don C. Johnson. jr.. was born in Springville on the 27th day of November. 1876. His education was acquired at the Hungerford academy and at the Collegiate and Sheldon-Jackson College in Salt Lake City. His labors have been varied. having done some farming. timbering and newspaper work.

Mr. Johnson's enlistment in the Spanish-American war dates from April 30. 1898. and his service was in the Philippines as a member of Battery B. Utah Volunteers. under Captain F. A. Grant. and for meritorious services was made corporal. He was in command of a gun section in Gen. McArthur's flying column in its advance to Malolos and San Fernando in 1899.

***

WILLIAM F. GIBSON.

William Franklin Gibson was born in Door County. Wisconsin, May 20, 1870, and came to Springville in 1895. He grew up and was educated on a farm, learning the printer's trade at a later period. Mr. Gibson has been connected with The Springville Independent in various capacities about five years and is an all 'round newpaperman.

ERRATA

On page 40, 2nd column, line 2, should read "Joseph D. Reynolds" instead of "James D. Reynolds."

Page 41, 2nd column, line 34, "bi-ennial" instead of "semi-annual."

Page 41, 2nd column, line 49, "1857-8" instead of "1587 7."

Page 45, 1st column, line 34, "$3,000" instead of "$,000."

Page 62, 1st column, line 34, "road built through Hobble Creek canyon in 1865."

Page 62, 2nd column, line 34, "Jacob Houtz" instead of "Lyman S. Wood."

Page 82, 2nd column, line 19, "1869-71" instead of "1872-3."

Page 110, 1st column, line 3, "1873-89" instead of "1863-89"

DATE DUE

992

1993